J. CAMERON PEDDIE

The Forgotten Talent

God's Ministry of Healing

Collins
FONTANA BOOKS

First published in Great Britain by the Oldbourne Book Co. Ltd., 1961
First issued in Fontana Books, 1966

THE FORGOTTEN TALENT

For more than thirty years J. CAMERON PEDDIE was a minister in Glasgow's Gorbals where he organised youth clubs, helped to settle group feuds, and brought help to innumerable families of various creeds and races. In 1942 he began to prepare for the ministry of healing, and his influence in this field has been felt by many. Today, over a hundred ministers of the Church of Scotland are following his example.

To the glory of God and in gratitude to Him for Netta, my wife, and for our children, Rosalind, Richard and Carol and for their families, all of whom have surrounded me with love and happiness and whose encouragement has made possible this book and the work that went into its making

PREFACE

Science is knowledge, perceived, understood and reduced to a system of facts acceptable to the human
mind. Within its own sphere the system is sound and
fruitful, but the sphere's ambit is limited.

The totality of truth is infinite and cannot be mea-
sured. Aspects of it, however, have been compre-
hended, but only in flashes of Divine Revelation.
Such Revelation is given to few because there have
been relatively few throughout history conditioned to
receive it.

Once received, consideration and credit must be
given to evidence and the communication may be
passed on by the recipient but it may be incapable of
demonstration or trial and may deny the laws of
science as we understand them.

Such an apparent denial of accepted scientific truth
by Divine Revelation is well illustrated in the following pages by the remarkable experiences of the Rev.
J. Cameron Peddie. Mr. Peddie is a well-known and
much loved figure throughout the poorer districts of
the City of Glasgow. He ministers to all who ask his
help regardless of their colour or creed and frequently
this takes him far beyond the boundary of his own
parish and indeed sometimes into distant towns.

He possesses a keen, analysing, objective mind and
always seeks a natural explanation for any phenome-
non before attributing it to Divine intervention. This
is particularly so in regard to the effects of his healing
ministrations which have frequently astounded the
many medical practitioners with whom he works in

the closest co-operation. Sometimes his intervention accelerates the patients' response to treatment, but in many cases where medical measures have failed he has brought about a complete reversal of a hopeless prognosis.

Again the laws of science appear to be denied or perhaps they are deviated by the intervention of providence. Whatever the explanation, the results are good and it is gratifying to know that many of the Clergy to-day are following the lead of this man of vision who has enriched the lives of those fortunate enough to know him and stimulated the Church to a reappraisal of its function and duties to the community.

A. D. MOFFAT

L.R.C.P. (Edinburgh), L.R.F.P.S. (Glasgow),
Pathologist, Glasgow

CONTENTS

CHAPTER I

NOT SINCE PENTECOST

During the Glasgow Fair of July, 1942, I was fending
for myself while Netta, my wife, and our children
were at the family country cottage four miles beyond
East Kilbride, near the foot of the Strathaven hills. I
could not stay long with them because at that time of
the year there is a plethora of weddings in the Gorbals;
it was quite usual to have twelve in one afternoon and
evening and this year was no exception.

What with sick visits and marriages I had not
found time to have a meal since breakfast and now it
was evening and I somewhat wearily went to my last
wedding of the day, to a hall in Thornliebank, a
suburb of Glasgow. I was tired and very hungry and
when the wedding feast came on, I ate ravenously of
the steak pie. It tasted rather queer, but I hoped for
the best, fearing no ill results. When I reached home
about ten o'clock I was conscious of a pain in my
back. I was sure it would be temporary—indigestion
perhaps—but there was a shadow of fear in my mind
that it might be ptomaine poisoning. As the pain
increased my fears intensified and I made myself a
cup of tea but it brought no relief. Then I had a hot
bath but still there was no relief and when I went to
bed with an intensely hot water-bottle the agony,
centred in my back, was almost unbearable.

Gradually it became difficult and still more difficult
to breathe and I turned and tossed and sat up in bed,
trying every device I could think of to secure relief.

By two o'clock no relief came and I was desperate and decided I had been poisoned.

What was I to do, ill and alone in the house? It was wartime, the black-out was on and no doctor or taxi would come out at such an hour. I decided the only sane thing to do was to go on foot to the Victoria Infirmary.

At 2.30 a.m. I left home scarcely able to stand let alone walk. It was just less than a mile to the infirmary but as I stumbled along by the side of Queen's Park, I wished fervently that a policeman would appear and help me. Not a soul was to be seen or heard. I sat on the pavement and how long I rested I cannot say. I either fell asleep or lost consciousness. When I realised again that I had to get to hospital, making a desperate effort, sometimes walking, sometimes crawling, I reached the entrance to the Victoria and told the porter I had been poisoned. It was 5 a.m. and I was rushed inside and immediately assured that I had not been poisoned but was suffering from something else.

Put to bed in a public ward, I was given an injection which eased the pain; I slept till 11 a.m. and wakened to hear a doctor say: " He hasn't moved." My pain was gone and the doctors and nurses gave me the kindest possible treatment and constant attention. But when the administrative authorities discovered I was a minister, they felt I could afford to pay my way and transferred me to a room in the Annexe which accommodated four patients.

After clinical examination it was discovered that the trouble was centred in my gall-sack and the surgeon informed me that it could be temporarily cured by medical treatment without surgery, but would be sure to return sooner or later. I asked him to operate, which he did successfully. After the operation I felt very fit and started convalescence with confidence.

I looked around me and made friends with a young man of thirty years, not so fortunate as I. He had been operated on : it was not successful and he was being sent home to die. But he did not know it. As I lay in that room talking to the doomed man, my mind began to dwell on the Ministry of Divine Healing as described in the Bible. The doctors and surgeons had done all they could for him but their " all " was not enough. If only the Church, I thought, could step in now in the strength and power of her Lord, his health would be restored. Should his minister take up the healing work from there or could I do it?

We could pray with him, comfort and help him to accept his fate. But if Jesus were here what would He do? I knew that with a word or the touch of His hand Jesus would heal him.

I could not forget my hospital friend and it was with a determination to look into this healing aspect of the Church's duties and do something about it that I left hospital. When I returned to work some weeks later, the first thing I did was seek guidance from the Bible. My thoughts had flown to Our Lord's commission : " Preach the Gospel, heal the sick." We had been taught as Divinity Students that the second half of the commission was meant for the Disciples only and their immediate followers, and not for us. But, I argued with myself—if the second half of that commission does not apply to us, how do we know the first half does? The words make sense only if we believe Our Lord's commission is indivisible and act on that belief. Our responsibility is both to preach *and heal*.

The next discovery I made from the Bible was that the purpose of the signs and wonders expressed in healing services is to confirm the words we preach. In the last verse of Mark's Gospel (and it does not matter who wrote that verse : it is true) it is unequivocally stated : " The Disciples went everywhere preaching the word with *signs* following."

This, I realised, was where my ministry had failed. I had not been giving the Lord an opportunity to confirm the word I was preaching. It was true that the Holy Spirit could take the word and press it home to the heart and conscience of the hearers and thus make converts. That would confirm the word, but, alas, how seldom it happened. The Healing Ministry seemed a readier and more effective instrument for the Holy Spirit to use in the Disciples' days. To anticipate somewhat, I now can say from experience that it is one thing to preach an eloquent sermon on a text such as " My God shall supply all your need " and stop with the sermon. But it is quite another thing to preach that same sermon and then, as you proceed from the pulpit to the vestry, find yourself followed by an old lady with an agonising headache who asks for a service of Divine Healing, and in a few minutes her pains are gone !

Quite recently, for example, one of my elders, coming to church, was seized with an attack of lumbago so severe he had to stay in an anteroom till the service was over. At the end of the service two of his fellow elders almost carried him, weeping from pain, into the vestry and asked me to give him a healing service. In five minutes the man's pains had gone and he was completely cured. What is more, the word I had preached had been confirmed. That is what every preacher should be able to do.

During my initial approach to this ministry my attention was directed to the healing work carried on in Glasgow by Spiritualist mediums. This, as you will see later on, was providential. The wife of a Jewish neighbour and friend was suffering from cancer in the throat. She had undergone one operation and her doctor wanted her to go through another as the external wound was not healing. She and her husband were distraught.

Before the war, my Jewish friend had escaped from the Nazis and I had done a little to help him rehabilitate himself. As a result he came to confide in me and to place a high value on my opinion on any matter that affected him.

He told me that he had heard of a spiritualist, a lady medium, who was doing wonderful healing work. Did I think it wise and right for him to take his wife to her, he asked? "No," I replied. "Have nothing to do with her." During my ministry in the High Church, Aberdeen, I should explain, I had investigated spiritualism, and been unimpressed. Hence my scepticism. Some time later my friend returned with the same question, and I gave the same answer. But when he came a third time, I saw he was very distressed and I said: "Yes, for goodness' sake take your wife to the woman. If she does her no good, she will do her no harm."

He took her, and my wife and I awaited the result with interest. To our surprise the sick woman's wound began to heal and in six months was closed. I do not suppose the doctors would admit a complete cure, but the lady is now well and hearty after some twenty years.

Here was something for us ministers to investigate. My wife, Netta, for ten years had been suffering intense pain from fibrositis and our son Richard, then twelve, was a victim of bronchial asthma. So I asked my Jewish friends to arrange an appointment for us to see the lady who had helped them. She received us with sympathy and kindness, telling us the touching story of how she was led, through the death of an infant son, to take up the work.

She offered herself to God for the work and after several years, when she had almost given up hope of being accepted, found she was able to heal under the control of a discarnate spirit. Having told us her story she sat on an ordinary chair and we waited to see what would happen. Gradually the expression on her face changed and the features seemed to alter, taking on an eastern appearance. She was under trance.

" Good morning," said the spirit and she offered up one of the most beautiful prayers I ever have heard.

We felt ourselves in the presence of an angel—certainly not a devil. She laid hands on my wife. She did this for about half an hour and gave our son the same service. My wife's pain disappeared for the first time in ten years and the boy's condition greatly improved.

My investigations into the beliefs and practice of the Spiritualist Movement and the conclusions I reached could not be related in detail here so I will merely write that the Spiritualists investigated were gracious and kindly and welcomed me and my friends to their meetings, services and seances. While it became evident, in due course, that they aimed to win us as converts to their beliefs we, on the other hand, hoped to win them back to Christianity. But they had no place in their creed or practice for Jesus Christ as Redeemer.

Orthodox Spiritualists regard Christ merely as a prophet. At their seances they asked me to open the meeting and I led them in prayer as if they were ordinary church folk. Many of them thanked and assured me that when I prayed in the names of Jesus Christ there seemed to be a different atmosphere in the room or hall. But no conversions either way occurred. I did, however, make several discoveries that must be stated here as they influenced me in my approach to the Ministry of Divine Healing.

First: these Spiritualist mediums, when sincere, were actually healing or, at any rate, giving relief to the sufferers who sought their aid.

Second: the vast majority of their patients were members of our Christian Churches. This meant that the Christian Church, by neglecting the Healing Ministry, was driving its members to Spiritualism. If our ministers knew how many of their flock go to Spiritualist mediums for services, they would get a shock.

Third: these Spiritualist Mediums were healing in the name and power of familiar spirits—not necessarily evil spirits, but discarnate ones.

Fourth: it was touching to see how earnestly, patiently and wholeheartedly they sat in silence waiting to be controlled by familiar spirits. I thought as I observed their endeavour of complete surrender to these spirits, that if we ministers would exercise as much patience and devote as much time in offering ourselves to the control of the Holy Spirit there would be such a spiritual reawakening in the Church as has not happened since Pentecost.

By this time I was aflame with jealousy for the honour of my Lord. Here was a movement that was doing good work for humanity professedly in the name and power of familiar spirits which the Ministry of the Church should be doing in the name of Jesus Christ. Something drastic had to be done to correct the gross omission of which the Church was guilty and I resolved to do something about it. I could offer only myself to God so I entered into what I regard as a private, personal covenant with Him. I did not know whether He would recognise this covenant but I would leave it in His hands. The terms on my side were absolute surrender of my personality, body, mind and spirit into His hands to be moulded and transformed in any way necessary to make me a suitable instrument for receiving and transmitting His healing grace to the needy. It was clear that a process of complete sanctification, cleansing and purifying was necessary to make this possible under the power of the Holy Spirit. I therefore set apart a room in our home as a personal Sanctuary reserved exclusively for prayer and meditation, and waiting upon the Lord. Each night I went there. And, so under God, my ministry of healing began.

CHAPTER 2

THE BORROWING DAYS

The Lord said to Habakkuk, " write the vision and make it plain upon tables, that he may run that readeth it." Time and again those words have rung in my ears but never till now have I felt it possible to yield to the accompanying impulse to write the simple and strange story of how and why I was led into the practice of the Ministry of Divine Healing. I have done this work for thirteen years but hitherto I have regarded the inevitable impulse to write of it as one of the many temptations associated with it. I have often related the story of my experiences leading up to this ministry, especially to groups of ministers and also at Healing Conferences. After such talks I invariably have been asked : " When are you going to write a book to help and guide us?" Some have graciously added : " We are waiting for it." But my answer was always, " I have no time for writing books. I am too busy doing work which the Lord has given me to do."

But recently the words, " Write the vision and make it plain upon tables, that he may run that readeth it," have remained with me more persistently. The sands of time are running out with me—as indeed with all of us. I am amongst " the borrowing days ", as the old folk used to call the years beyond three score and ten.

" Write that story of yours for the sake of younger men. You are getting old—and one never knows," said a retired missionary from abroad after hearing me speak at a Healing Conference nine years ago. Be that as it may, a few months ago I resolved before God in my heart to find at least one hour in the day to devote to this task.

" A good man's steps are ordered of the Lord." So says the Psalmist. I cannot claim to be a good man. Who can? But I can and do claim that at all vital points in my life, my steps have been ordered of the Lord. I look back across the years and see myself a little boy of seven joining other children who are playing at " Gospel Meetings ". We sat in a circle on the ground and on his knees in the middle an older child was acting the preacher. We others were entranced as we listened to the boy gospeller; red in the face from the vehemence with which he proclaimed his message, he thumped the ground with his fists to emphasise his points. The only emphatic word I remember to-day is the word " God ", which constantly he reiterated. I do recall however the solemn appeal I myself made to that same God. It was perhaps my first original prayer : " O God make me a preacher of the Gospel like this boy."

Seven years passed and I was fourteen, the critical stage when a boy then had to decide whether to continue studies or go out into the world to make a livelihood. Already I had exceeded school-leaving age by two years and I still wished to preach the Gospel in the Ministry of the Church. The pulpit was the goal of my life and the terms of the covenant I proposed to establish with God were simple. If by divine help plus hard work I could secure a County Council Bursary, allocated in those days, not on the basis of mere selection from a number of applicants, but on the competitive conditions of scholastic endeavour, I would dedicate myself to the Ministry of the Church. But if I could not win a bursary then my path in life would take another direction.

In due course I succeeded in winning a senior County bursary of £20 per annum for three years and this was sufficient to cover the expenses of higher education. Hitherto the foundation of my education had been laid in Largue Public School, Forgue, Aberdeenshire, whose devoted Headmaster, John Gray, took great pride in bringing on the " lad-o-pairts ". He had many distinguished scholars to his credit and he tutored me half an hour before school opened each morning and kept me half an hour after it closed, to add me to his roll of honour.

Having won the bursary I now felt myself to have made a " bargain " with God, whose existence and real presence I never doubted in those days.

But when I contemplated leaving the calm security, protection and guardianship of my country home for the great city of Aberdeen with its famous Gordon's College, the nursery of so many first bursars, with temptations which I had not so far encountered, I was filled with misgivings as to whether I would stand the test or go down under the heel of the world's wickedness. Prayer brought me courage.

Carrying home the milk one evening from a neighbouring farm, passing through a field by the old home, I was engaged in my usual meditations and prayers, a sort of constant conversation with God, a habit I had developed on my lonely four-mile walk to school along highways, byways and forest paths. Suddenly a verse of Scripture flashed across my mind as a very message uttered by God. " Commit thy way unto the Lord. Trust also in Him and He shall bring it to pass." (Ps. 37.5).

So early I discovered that God speaks to men and boys in every crisis of life, not in the audible syllables the prophets heard, but in the recorded words of old. God never wastes time, energy or thought. What already is recorded for our learning He does not repeat. He helps us to recall it but he gives it that peculiar emphasis and special shade of meaning in our minds which make it " pat " for the occasion.

The words came to me as I contemplated in fear and uncertainty, the temptations to which I would be exposed in the city, and the prospects of success or failure in my chosen career.

That text was my mainstay all through my subsequent checkered career.

Three more years of hard work with high thinking and sober living at Gordon's College, Aberdeen, and I won two other bursaries of twenty pounds each per annum for four years. This money enabled me to " leap another wall " and enter the University. But those three years left their mark upon me. Financial difficulties had caused me to live on two meals a day and meagre meals they were. Every morning as I left my lodging my prayer had been, " Lord Jesus be my schoolmate to-day, my companion and friend." Never for a single moment did I doubt the answer to that prayer. Hitherto my faith had been that of a little child—the simple unquestioning trust in God's Word that my mother taught me. This simple faith, however, was shaken as knowledge increased and other opinions which challenged the goodness and very existence of God came into my mind. This new knowledge relegated most of what had been the mainstay of my mind and soul to the realm of myth and legend.

So shattering was the effect of my University education and associations that on graduating I was in doubt as to whether I should proceed to the Divinity Hall and decided to do a year's teaching in a private Civil Service College in order to gain time for further thought.

Had I done this I think it unlikely that I would have entered on the course to the ministry. The entrance examination to the Divinity Hall was to take place in September, 1910, but I had done no preparation as I did not intend to take it. But on the night before examination day, with all thought of proceeding on the path to the pulpit now fast receding I was visited by a College friend, a minister's son, who wished to talk with me. This lad had determined that I should not be lost to the Church and after long argument he succeeded in persuading me that my earlier sense of call to the ministry must be heeded and obeyed. The result of his advice was that, without any special preparation, I sat the examination next day and passed. Thus once again my " steps were ordered of the Lord ". My friend, I believe, was a messenger from God.

It was to be expected that life at the Divinity Hall and the training received there would dissolve all my doubts, clarify my views and show me a clear path through the bewildering forest raised up by the Higher Criticism, scientific theories and the general atmosphere of scepticism which abounded in those days. But it would be nearer the truth to say that I left the seminary an intellectual pagan. Yet, in retrospect, I am aware that deep down, beneath all my accumulated learning and the intellectual scars that seared my soul, lay the shattered remains of the simple faith my mother had instilled, together with the unforgettable occasions on which the hand of The Living God had been laid upon me.

Was Christ still alive for me? Was there any Gospel left? Was I justified in proceeding to the work of the ministry of the church? Had I anything worthwhile to say? Such questions challenged me constantly.

On the 17th of May, 1917, between the hours of eleven and twelve, the day after my thirtieth birthday, I was ordained to the ministry in Kennoway United Free Church, Fifeshire, which was linked with Windygates United Free Church, a mile and a half away. Both churches were in low water but after I toiled hard amongst both young and old for three years, the empty pews filled.

By 1920 the churches each required a minister and I persuaded the local Presbytery that such an arrangement was necessary for the good of the communities. In order to speed the development I sent in my resignation and the Presbytery accepted it, both churches were declared vacant, and both gave me an unofficial call urging me to come back when the union was regularly dissolved. Meantime I felt I could do better work for my fellows as a doctor, and so, on leaving Fifeshire, I made my way to my old home in Forgue, Aberdeenshire, to wait there for the opening of the next Session in medicine at Aberdeen University.

During this brief period I was asked to fill for one Sunday the vacant pulpit of the High United Free Church in the city and there, to my surprise and dis-

comfiture, the congregation, through its leaders, asked
if I would accept a call. Once again I felt the hand
of God dragging me back into the ministry. " Surely
God has some special purpose in this for me. He
must need me in His Church ". So I ruminated, pon-
dering still another crisis of the soul. I found I could
not do other than accept.

Three years of successful ministry in Aberdeen were
followed by six years in Westbourne Church, Barr-
head. Then the Gorbals of Glasgow called and again
I was certain the Hand of God was in the business and
accepted.

In the Gorbals I soon realised that my real life-work
had begun. Cuninghame United Free Church had
been vacant for eighteen months. At the start of the
vacancy the congregation had approached me, but
family circumstances did not allow of my accepting.
After eighteen months, during which the congregation
failed to agree on calling a minister, they approached
me again. By then my family circumstances had
changed and I accepted this call. Two years later
Cuninghame Church, the Old Briggate Parish Church
and Hutchesontown Parish united under my ministry
and became Hutchesontown Parish.

I had been working as a minister in the Gorbals of
Glasgow for fourteen years and my work covered
three worlds.

First there was the ordinary congregational world
in which I ministered to a normal congregation of
mixed social classes consisting of some seven hundred
members.

Second there was the home mission world where I
and my workers moved amongst the poorer people,

decent respectable citizens who were lost to the church, chiefly because their poverty prevented them from attending services through lack of decent clothing. We made an appeal to these folk through personal visits and evangelistic endeavour expressed in Gospel tea meetings and the results were gratifying. Every year at least eighty responded to our appeal.

Third, there was the most wonderful and fascinating world of all, the underworld where the citizens of that grim realm look upon crime as an achievement, especially when they are not found out.

In the Gorbals of that time the lawless element was organised into gangs that engaged in crime and gang warfare. There were thirty such in the Gorbals, each consisting of some two hundred members, and by 1930 they had become a menace to the community as well as an insoluble problem to the Police.

I regarded gangsterism in Glasgow as primarily a social problem, the street battles, violent and deplorable as they were, as youthful frolics. Employment was scarce in those days and if idle, uneducated, and lively-minded youths are given only themselves for company and the streets as playgrounds inevitably they will be bored and out of that boredom find wild ways to express themselves. They did so in the Gorbals by banding together and by fighting they tried to demonstrate their individual and collective superiority to other persons and other gangs. It was the period of the American gangster film and very cheap tickets for afternoon cinema shows, which added what is called " glamour " to the whole silly business.

Silly it was but it also was serious. When one of the gang-fights started the public might be in the way. Missiles were thrown and often the innocent were

injured. Deaths had been caused, unwittingly, by
such fights. There was, however, I believe no real
criminal intention in the minds of the youths engaged.
They were victims of an environment which provided
no real outlet for their vitality and they were work-
less, their day-to-day lives purposeless.

My introduction to the gangsters came through my
getting in their way— or rather, more precisely, my
church getting in their way. There had been a big
professional football match, between Glasgow Rangers
F.C., and Glasgow Celtic F.C., and groups of lads
representing two factions clashed afterwards. I don't
know which team won, but the result, inevitably, was
found disagreeable by the supporters of the losers.
So they went to war and as their battle zone chose
the environs of my church.

Until then I was unaware that there were such
things as gangs in Glasgow as I took no interest in
police court news. But since my church figured in
the battle I studied the account of the proceedings
which followed the arrest of four youths who had
taken part in the mêlée; and I was struck by something that emerged in the questioning. It seemed, I
read, that local shopkeepers were being terrorised by
these lads. indeed one detective asserted, very truly
as I found out, that when he questioned local merchants about the gangs " they went white with fear ".

I felt I must do some investigating on my own part
for if these lads did not come to church it was the
Church's duty to go to them. First I followed the
professional example of the detectives and visited the
shopkeepers. From them I got largely the same reaction as the police had received. The only one, indeed,
who gave me a forthright answer curiously enough

was a man who had more reason to fear violence than most folk; he was an ex-soldier who suffered badly from shell-shock. He told me that the gangs were intimidating quiet-living citizens, and merchants in particular.

I then took a walk around the more thickly inhabited street-corners and chatted to the men I found standing about. Like the merchants they were reluctant to talk about the gangs. But after I left them the word went around that " the minister " was interested and a deputation of parents came to me after service the following Sunday. They told me that they could no longer stand the strain imposed on them by their adventurous children, asked my help and I promised to do what I could.

I also promised, within me, that I should go and live with these poor violent lads, mixing with them as the Master had done, trying to emulate His spirit and attitude, simply to do for them and be with them as He might if He were here. And I'd mention nothing of religion, for they were not, by any means, all of my own persuasion.

By a stroke of luck my annual holiday of one month began then and I had plenty of time to give my new congregation. It was the finest holiday I ever have spent. The Gorbals is a first-class holiday resort for those whom its salubrious atmosphere suits; it rejuvenated me in a way that prophesied the mission now closest to my heart, the heart which was the seat of my personal trouble at that time.

I was suffering from a minor cardiac disease and my doctor had given me strict orders to take extreme care of myself, not to overwork, to walk slowly upstairs, etc., to rest as often as possible. But here was this call to help the street-gangs and I knew it would make big demands on my strength.

I thought the matter over and soon came to a decision. I told the Good Physician that if I was to do His work He would have to do His part and fix my heart for me. It has never missed a beat since.

The leading gang, and the wildest, was known as the South Side Stickers. They had in their record six gang murders and when I took them in hand and transformed their gang into a club with the gang-leader becoming a club-leader, one of their number was imprisoned for murder. The club idea caught on amongst the gangsters and within two years I had organised thirty clubs in the Gorbals, housed in vacant shops, pubs and empty factories (of which there were plenty in those days). Unemployment, I insist, was the root cause of the gangsterdom of those days.

To try and find a positive answer to the problem I organised work schemes, a firewood factory, an advertising agency using bill distribution throughout the whole city, a vinegar bottling factory and, for the women, a knitwear factory. Now after thirty years, I confidently can say that over seventy-five per cent of those wild men have been for many long years decent, respectable citizens.

Quite recently I was making my way home in a tramcar and when it reached my stop I got out and crossed the road. I looked back at the tram and was surprised to see it still at the stop. Then I saw the driver running after me. He was " Pug ", one of my Stickers whom I had not seen for years. He had left his tramcar, crowded with passengers anxious to get home, in order to thank me for what I had done for him in those early days of his life.

" Pug " had married many years before and had a son at the University and one of his daughters about to sit her matriculation examination. This good man alone was worth all the time and strength and money I had spent in the underworld of those days.

The story of my experiences in the underworld where the South Side Stickers reigned supreme would require a volume to itself, but I have given these few details of my social work in order to discourage those who may read the following account of my Healing Ministry from dubbing me a mystical dreamer with no practical capacity.

I should like to stress the enrichment of spiritual experience I derived from my work amongst these gangsters. What supported, encouraged and gave me the necessary patience and courage, as I worked early and late amongst these men, was a sense of call to the work, a consciousness of the Divine Presence which at times was vivid. There also was the repeated experience of answers to prayer. Always I relied upon the promises given by the Great Master and He never failed me. I faced many crises, many dangerous situations arose, but His Word stood sure, as the Bible declares. The following incident which is only one amongst many, will illustrate what I mean.

When I took up this work one of the South Side Stickers, a lad I shall name Harry, was in prison. He had been sentenced at the age of eighteen to seven years' penal servitude for killing another lad in a gang fight. Good conduct gained Harry two years' remission and he was released after serving five years. He had gone to prison a fresh young lad; he was released with hair as white as an old man's. We gave him a great welcome, organised a special " At Home " for him and he was astonished but pleased to find his former friends no longer gangsters but happy members of a club. Soon I found him a job and he settled down, did well and became a most helpful member. But one Sunday night after the services were over, when we were holding a business meeting of the club in the Church Hall, someone proposed that a young man named John, waiting outside, should be made a member and I asked if there were any objections.

" Yes, sir," said Harry, " I object to that man becoming a member of our club."

" What have you against him ?"

He sat down and gave no explanation.

" Do any of you chaps know what trouble is between them ?" I asked the meeting.

" Yes, sir, we know all about it. It's a personal matter, sir, a personal matter."

" Well," I said, " will you ask John to come into the vestry with me and we will try and settle this personal matter. You come too, Harry."

I went into the vestry, the two boys followed and I shut the door to ensure privacy. They stood before me quiet and sullen : Harry would not even look at John.

" What have you got against this man ?" I asked.

Pointing at John over his shoulder with his thumb, he replied, looking straight into my eyes :

" Sir, this man gave me away at my trial. On this man's evidence I was condemned. On this man's evidence I might have been hanged. I'm not finished with him yet."

I was conscious of crisis, and put up a silent prayer as I looked at them both, reminding my Master He had promised that in time of crisis He would guarantee that the Holy Spirit would put the appropriate words upon our lips. He did and I asked John if the accusation was true.

" Yes, it is true," he admitted.

" Why did you do it, John?" I asked. " You know that in our code of honour we do not inform on an enemy, not to speak of a friend. Isn't that so?"

" Yes," was the reply.

" Then why did you do it?"

" Well, sir," he argued. " I was young then and I was on oath and I felt I had to speak the truth."

I faced a difficult situation as a minister and I cannot remember all I said, but I know that the words were given me. I talked for about ten minutes gradually turning the argument into John's favour and pointing out to Harry how dangerous it was for him to harbour these feelings of revenge.

When I reached that point I became conscious of another presence in the room. Three of us had entered the vestry, but now there were four, just as in the Bible story. They felt it too and tears ran down Harry's cheeks as he held out a hand to John, and John, with responding tears, grasped it. There they were, the ex-convict and the man whose evidence had sent him away, reconciled. We returned to the club meeting, and when I announced the result of our conference, the applause was tremendous and none gave John a heartier welcome into the club membership than Harry. They became close friends.

There are some who may question the morality of the way I handled the situation. Wasn't John right in giving evidence on oath against a killer? Of course he was right but my work among the Gorbals Gangs was not only to *prevent* crime—I was as much— indeed more concerned with rehabilitating those who had grievously sinned. I recognised no varying standards of morality or Christianity; frequently I had to act as a judge and in many cases I felt that my means must primarily be persuasive, towards the redemptive end—I never had cause to regret the outcome.

This is but one of many incidents in my work in the underworld which confirmed for me the essential message of the Bible and served as a measure of preparation for my ministry of healing which demanded a still sharper edge on my faith.

CHAPTER 3

THE NAIL IN MY PALM

The room I set aside as a sanctuary was as far from the traffic of the outside world as the house would permit. I also set apart one hour in each day for meditation and soon discovered that the best time to engage in this method of spiritual discipline was from eleven to midnight. Then, all interruptions ceased; no phone or doorbell disturbed me, no domestic activities intruded and I could feel entirely away from the world, even from the thought of it, and alone with God. In time I began to think of this as " my hour of Watch with Christ ". I remembered His words to the disciples " Could you not watch with me for one hour?" and discovered there is a special significance in the period of one hour in our relationship with God. It seems that our personality is so constituted that we are capable of being *vividly* conscious of the Divine Presence for about sixty minutes—no more at a given time.

Thus to keep watch with Christ is to do more than just pray. The time for prayer has passed and one is reduced to silence in the presence of God. The sense of that presence is so definite that one knows exactly, to the very minute, without any watch or clocks, when the Hour ends. I have discovered that this feature of spiritual experience has an application much wider and beyond the Hour of Watch. If, for example, someone asks me to pray for a special case and I fix the time of joint prayer, say ten minutes or half an hour, when I go into my sanctuary for that period of prayer, I do not need a watch to tell me when it is up. At the very moment of its passing, the sense of being in close contact with the Divine Power ceases and there is a strange feeling of emptiness. And this does not happen only in my sanctuary. To develop thus the sense of the Divine Presence is the essential duty of every Christian, but especially for those who wish to do special work for Him.

On entering the sanctuary I review the day's work in His presence submitting it to Him for approval. I beg forgiveness and cleansing and then ask for grace to sift the motives that urge me towards the Healing Ministry, seeking with all possible earnestness deliverance from even the suggestion of selfishness.

In the beginning I realised that I myself must be my first offering. Thus every night I offered Him my whole personality, my body, mind, and spirit for the high and holy purpose. The surrender of the whole personality became the most important feature of my preparation and it had to be tackled in a practical way.

Instead of offering in a vague general way my body, I went over my every physical feature, mentioning each by name, bones, muscles, sinews, glands, nerves, etc., indeed every cell, asking the Creator to re-create every part of me as He saw fitting in order to render me a suitable instrument in His Hands for the purpose in view.

With my mind I followed the same routine, detailing its every aspect, memory, imagination, intellect, will, etc.; then I offered my spirit about which I knew nothing, except that it must be my real Ego, but which, with all its mysterious powers, is known to Him only.

Such was my method of special spiritual discipline; such my effort to become a medium of the spirit that was in Jesus Christ. This endeavour was not limited to my hour of watch. It also demanded a thorough search of the Bible for every reference to the Healing Ministry and for every passage in it that offered guidance. Such study of the Word, with prayer and meditation, often continued through the night, and always when I was alone during the day my thoughts reverted to spiritual matters. Life became in large measure a walk in heavenly places with Christ by my side.

For a whole year I carried out these daily tasks as faithfully as I could, always expecting something to happen that would make clear to me that the Lord recognised the personal private covenant I had tried to enter into with Him and call me to this Ministry. I could not expect such a call as Isaiah or Peter or Paul experienced; but I believed that God might in some more simple way let me hear His " Whom shall I send ", with my own response " Here am I, send me ".

But no such thing happened and I continued my special programme for a second year. But still there was no call other than my own wishful thinking.

A third year passed, then a fourth with the same result and I was tempted to give up. But, under the impulse of what must have been the Holy Spirit, for no other power could have sufficed to keep me going, I regularly continued my routine. Before the end of the fifth year something happened.

The sign came on the 17th of May, 1947, between the hours of 11 a.m. and noon, exactly thirty years to the hour after my ordination. I had been ordained to the Holy Ministry on the 17th of May, 1917, between the hours of 11 a.m. and noon in that dear Fifeshire church. It was the day after my thirtieth birthday. My life has been divided into equal periods of thirty years from my birth to ordination; thirty years after my ordination I received the call to the Healing Ministry. I have a hope—perhaps flattering to myself—that the Lord may grant me a third period of thirty years to exercise this Ministry and help re-establish it as a regular feature of every minister's work.

During the months April to July, 1947, my wife Netta and our three children, Rosalind, Richard and Carol, our youngest child, were living in our cottage on the heights towards the Strathaven hills. Rosalind had been ill and when she was almost convalescent, her doctor, a lady, discovered she had been suffering from pleurisy. The condition was dangerous and the doctor advised that a sojourn in fresh hill air was essential to the child's complete recovery.

Rose Cottage and its high situation met her need, and as it was only twelve miles from Glasgow, I could travel to my duties in church and parish with ease and comfort, but for the most part I preferred to stay by myself in our Glasgow home.

This particular day I was alone and between eleven and twelve was preparing lunch. What happened might have been expected in the sanctuary, a Cathedral or on some piece of holy ground. But it happened as I stood at the sink in the kitchen paring potatoes, a knife in one hand, a potato in the other.

What my thoughts were I cannot remember but I have no doubt that being alone I was talking to the Father about the work I wished to do. Whatever thoughts engaged my attention, suddenly I felt myself gripped by a strange benevolent power that filled me with an unspeakable sense of happiness. I seemed to be drawn up out of the body and did not know where I was, whether " in the body or out of it ". It was supreme and final bliss! Joy filled my heart and over-flowed in tears, helplessly I cried, like a child, the tears pouring from my eyes. All I could say was " Father, oh Father ". I was the Prodigal Son arriv-ing home and the Father had fallen on my neck and was kissing me. I had reached, I knew, the home of ultimate truth and all things were clear and plain. All doubts vanished. Every question-mark was erased and I knew, I simply knew, that God is and that He rewards all who diligently seek Him.

That experience verified for me many Bible texts formerly somewhat obscure and almost impossible to believe, and lit them with new meaning. There is the strange experience Paul records in II Corinthians 12, vv. 2-4 : " I knew a man in Christ above fourteen years ago (whether in the body, I cannot tell : or whether out of the body, I cannot tell : God knoweth) such an one caught up to the third heaven. And I knew such a man (whether in the body, or out of the body, I cannot tell : God knoweth). How that he was caught up into paradise, and heard unspeakable words which it is not possible for a man to utter."

I can now *believe* that as an actual experience of Paul. Then there is another text, somewhat obscure, yet literally true, to them that have had the experience. Romans 8, v. 15 : " For ye have not received the spirit of bondage again to fear; but ye have received the Spirit of adoption, whereby we cry; ABBA; FATHER!"

These were the only words I could cry and they were uttered involuntarily, and in spite of myself as I wept, " Father; Oh Father ". When I thought of the sheer joy and pleasure of the experience I recalled Psalm 16, v. 11. " In thy presence is fulness of joy; at thy right hand there are pleasures for evermore."

I recalled too the saying of Jesus that His fellowship with His Disciples and the words He spoke were meant to enable them to taste His joy, that their joy might be full. Was this the full joy He was referring to? I certainly was full of joy and running over.

My first reaction to the experience was the thought; " This was God indicating to me that He had accepted my offer. It was His call to the Ministry of Healing." Such, I write, was my conviction. But the devil of doubt, like all other devils, never is far from the mind of man. I began to analyse the experience and I felt it was beyond human comprehension; but I could ask myself questions about it.

Was it real, factual experience? Or was it the exercise of an overheated imagination? Was it wishful thinking? Or was I—as the sceptical psychologist might assert—an epileptic who, unknown to myself, had been suffering from the malady for sixty years? Was I a victim of mental derangement and qualifying for a mental hospital, or was it the devil himself?

I could not say what it was if not a baptism of the Holy Spirit. But experiences are like personalities— " by their fruits ye shall know them ". Only one Power could clear up the situation for me—the Power that gave the experience—God himself.

In the midst of my perplexity I remembered the Bible story of Gideon to whom an angel appeared as he threshed his corn and announced that God had chosen him to do special work for His people. Gideon listened attentively and doubtfully and after the Divine messenger had gone, he began to question the reality of his experience. Was it real? Was it truly a messenger and a message from God? Gideon was nonplussed, so he asked God to give him the two signs of the fleece, now wet, now dry, to prove the reality of the experience and truth of the message. God gave him the signs he asked. Formerly under the influence of the Liberal Theology of my day I had considered that incident merely as legend or myth; now I believe it really happened. It is the kind of thing that can happen when one is in the Spirit; for to be in the Spirit means to have one's spiritual faculties operating under the power of the Holy Ghost and under that Power all things are possible. Had others been with Gideon when the angel came to him, they would have seen and heard nothing unless they too had been " in the Spirit ".

I reflected on Gideon's experience and it occurred to me that there was no reason why the Lord should not give me two signs that would verify the reality and purpose of the experience I had passed through.

I knew that in religious circles it is regarded as evidence of weak faith to ask for such signs. " Did not Jesus say," they argue, " this wicked and idolatrous generation seeketh after a sign but no sign shall be given it," and they stop there. But Jesus did not stop there. His actual words are " No sign shall be given it except the sign of Jonas. For as Jonas was three days and three nights in the whale's belly, so shall the Son of Man be three days and three nights in the heart of the earth." Here he points to His coming resurrection as a sign and what sign could be greater or more effective in dispelling doubt?

The fact of the matter is that every new advance that was made in the progress of revealed truth, as recorded in the Bible, was heralded or confirmed by a sign of some kind. Even the shepherds of the first Christmas were given a sign to dispel their doubts and verify their experience. "This shall be a sign unto you. Ye shall find the babe wrapt in swaddling clothes lying in a manger." But in addition to all that, may it not be that those who boast of a faith that is independent of signs may in reality not have sufficient faith to ask for a sign in case they might not get one? Finally when Jesus said to Thomas "Blessed are they who have not seen and yet have believed," the implication is that those who both see and believe are twice blessed.

Satisfying myself with these reflections I asked the Lord to give me two signs to verify the interpretation I had placed upon my experience. He gave me those signs but I had to wait for them. "If the vision tarry, wait for it," says Habakkuk.

For the first sign I had to wait three months. In order to complete Rosalind's recovery, on the specialist's advice, we spent the whole of August that year at Prestwick on the Ayrshire coast. August is my holiday month so I was able to accompany the family. We booked accommodation in the North Marina Hotel, close to the shore but as it was crowded with other holiday-makers, my son and I slept in a chalet in the grounds. This had its advantages as we could go out and in at any time of day or night without disturbing anyone. But for me there was one serious drawback. I had no means of creating a sanctuary where I could have my Hour of Watch with Christ. However, I soon found a glorious substitute. I discovered that from 11 p.m. till midnight a great stretch of sand by the beach was vacant and I could have it all to myself. The other holiday-makers then were in bed and I could walk alone with my Lord hearing nothing but the swish of the waters without and the sound of His voice within. At that time one particular thing worried me; if I should ever start the Ministry of Healing, how would I get it across to my fellow ministers.

If I were to tell my colleagues I was taking up this work, they might only laugh and think me insane. If I were to try to persuade them of the possibility of it, marshalling my arguments on the basis of Scripture, they very soon would argue me down. Yet my purpose was to get *all* ministers to take it up and the outlook seemed unpromising.

One night I was specially worried over the problem as my Hour of Watch ended. Thinking furiously I made my way across the sands to the chalet and just before I reached it, I was moved (I have now no doubt) by the Holy Spirit, to take a daring step. I know that it is neither lawful nor expedient to use the Bible as a book of magic, but I believe that in a crisis of the soul, or at some cross-roads of experience, God permits a man to do what I did.

As I approached the bedroom where my son was asleep, I said to God, " Father I still am in the dark and cannot see my way through this perplexing situation. How can I get this question of the Healing Ministry across to my brother ministers? When I enter my little bedroom I will open my Bible. Please let the first words I see be a message to guide me." I entered our room, sat down on my bed and stretched out my hand to open the Bible lying on the dressing-table. I pointed my finger on a verse and was about to read it, when three pages turned over singly, one after the other, as if moved by an unseen hand; they remained in a naturally impossible position above my pointing finger.

Still, despite my intense surprise, I did not move the finger but leaned forward and read Luke 21, v. 15: " I will give you a mouth and wisdom, which all your adversaries shall not be able to gainsay nor resist." This was on the last leaf that had turned over. So that was that problem settled, and the first of the two signs I had asked for.

For almost three months I waited for the second sign.

We returned to our Glasgow house at the end of August. The month had passed without a drop of rain—sunshine poured on us every day, which could not have been better arranged. Rosalind's cure was complete; the weather had revitalised the whole family, preparing us to face the coming winter's work with confidence. I resumed my regular routine of spiritual discipline—study of the Bible, almost constant prayer, walking the heavenly places with Christ, the atmosphere of prayer always blowing around my mind and above all my Hour of Watch alone in my Sanctuary.

Here I wish to emphasise that little word " *alone.*"

To develop our spiritual faculties to a high degree and practise the consciousness of the Divine Presence effectively, it is absolutely essential to have our Hour of Watch alone. Another personality present, no matter how close the spiritual affinity may be, acts as a disturbing factor to the consciousness of the Divine Presence.

Consider the method of Jesus. Time and again we read of Him going away into some quiet place to pray *alone*.

Even in Gethsemane when one would have thought the presence of spiritually kindred souls would have been helpful, we read of Him saying to His disciples, " Sit ye here, while I go and pray yonder." (Matthew 26, v. 36). After saying this we read that He took the three who were spiritually closest to Him, Peter, James and John, a little farther than the rest along that lonely road. But they had not gone far when He said to them " Tarry ye here and watch with me ". Then comes, " And He went a little farther."

Jesus could not allow any presence, not even these three, to come between Him and the Father or to disturb His consciousness of the Father's presence at that vital hour.

Then there is His very definite guidance for prayer given in Matthew 6, v. 6 : " But thou, when thou prayest, enter into thy closet, and when thou hast shut thy door, pray to thy Father which is in secret; and thy Father which seeth in secret shall reward thee openly." Make your sense of His Presence very vivid. Note the singulars " thou and thy ", also the shut door. Unquestionably the Hour of Watch must be shared by none but God Himself if we are to obtain the best results.

During the month following, September, a new development disturbed me deeply.

One night, having finished my Hour in the Sanctuary, which is in the basement of our three-storey house, as I reached the foot of the first stair, I felt it necessary to go down on my knees and speak to the Father about some idea that had occurred to me. As I did so, I felt myself charged with some power in effect very like electricity. The thrill of it filled my whole body but did not make me tremble and I was conscious of no sense of illness. I just felt charged with a strange force. Afterwards whenever I was alone in prayer, the same thing happened and as time went on and no ill effect appeared, I became convinced that the power had a spiritual origin. But was it from the region of spiritual light or spiritual darkness? I had been brought up in a sufficiently otherworldly atmosphere to make me fear that it might be of the devil. Only the Father could make the truth of the matter clear to me. But again I had to wait although my patience was threatening to give way. So one night, when I knelt down for a word of prayer before going to bed and this force seemed to be specially aggressive, almost in a spirit of impatience I prayed : " Oh, Father do something to let me know whether this power be of the light or of the darkness."

Then I did another daring thing, I suggested to God what He might do and so I continued my prayer : " Make this right arm and hand of mine move out of my control in an erratic way."

I watched to see whether my arm would begin to move and twitch in spite of my every effort to control it. But it did not move. God does not answer prayers to dictation. He answers them in a better way.

As I watched, still expecting my arm and hand to move out of control, I saw something very strange. My hand grew smaller, and became all bruised, as if it had been hammered. Then down from the roots of the first two fingers and between them, a large nail appeared driven in to the very head; from it blood trickled down the lines on the palm and round the wrist. I cannot say how long the vision lasted for time did not exist for me. This vision made things clear and I knew that the power of which I was conscious was of light and not darkness. This, I knew, was the power Jesus promised when He said: " Ye shall receive power after that the Holy Ghost is come upon you and ye shall be witnesses unto Me."

The decks were clear for action and the only remaining question was, with whom should I start? To which sufferer could I go up and say: " I am conscious of a Divine Healing Power. I will give you a service. The Lord will heal you through me "?

CHAPTER 4

CRADLE OF LIGHT

The " vision ", which truly was a point of Divine guidance came to me in May, 1948; in coming, it revealed God as utterly trustworthy, capable in everything and also as a Being Who has a sense of humour.

When I left it to the Holy Spirit to sift my motives for seeking to enter upon this Ministry, it became one of my chief concerns to avoid publicity. That meant avoiding reporters, journalists, and anyone likely to draw attention to me. But it pleased the Lord to arrange that I should start my Healing Ministry with a journalist's wife. " He that in heaven sits shall laugh," says the Bible. I am sure the situation appealed to God's sense of humour. He who endowed mankind with humorous propensities must Himself enjoy a joke. I am sure He enjoyed that one. There is a sense in which God is very human.

It happened that my wife and I visited two of our friends, an ecclesiastical journalist and his wife. We had not seen them for a long time and in recent years, unknown to us, the lady had been seriously ill, suffering from a heart condition which entailed three months' treatment by a Harley Street specialist. But still she suffered from pain about the heart, had gone deaf in the left ear, and, in addition, developed a general rheumatic condition, which made walking difficult. She could no longer accompany her husband as he went about his journalistic duties and this was a great source of sorrow as it had been such pleasure to her, sharing his work and responsibilities.

She had even attempted to secure the services of a spiritualist medium but in vain. While she poured out her sad story to us, she suddenly stopped and, looking at me with appealing eyes, said: "Mr. Peddie, I believe you could heal me if you liked!" I replied at once: "I believe I could."

The suddenness of the appeal, with the meaning that I could read into it, literally shook me. It made me too unsure of myself to give her a service that night. But we promised to return in a day or two which gave me time to calm myself and, through prayer and meditation, prepare with confidence for the step I was about to take. One thing was clear. The Lord actually had made arrangements for me to start this ministry by fixing the time, place and patient without me consciously doing anything about it—just as I had asked Him to do six months previously.

"If the vision tarry wait for it, because it will surely come." Habakkuk was right. It was a devastating experience and it shattered me into humility.

In a day or two we went back to our friend to give the service. It was a critical hour, but I felt prepared whatever might happen. The sick woman now was in bed and her husband and my wife were with us. I read a passage from Mark's Gospel appropriate to the occasion and briefly we prayed.

Then came the vital moment. I laid my hands upon her head and as I did so, there was given to me an experience that has not been repeated during all the years I have been exercising His ministry. I am sure the good Lord gave me that experience to encourage and instil in me the necessary confidence, lest I might doubt or hesitate on an occasion so fraught with significance for my future.

The patient was covered with blankets. But I saw her lying in a bath of golden light so indescribable in its beauty and brilliance, I can call it only the glory of God. She lay in that light during the whole half hour I was ministering and I felt God was thus making clear to me the reality of His presence and power. Never since then have I seen a patient so wrapped-up in God's Glory and Power. The Holy Spirit had opened my inner eye to enable me to see the Power at work on that occasion and I believe the same thing happens every time one is ministering in the name and power of Jesus Christ. But, like the two disciples on the road to Emmaus, our eyes are " holden ".

Within half an hour my friend's heart pain was gone, also her rheumatic pains, and she could hear better with the hitherto deaf ear than with the good one. She was, for the time being at any rate, completely cured.

I have never given a more effective service. But I got a fright for when I laid my hand upon the patient's heart, the pain became more acute, till it almost was unbearable. She got a fright too and I tried to lift my hand, but somehow, in spite of myself, I held it there, or it was held for me, till the pain died away.

Those were early days and I did not know what I know now; that the power administered by the Holy Spirit gradually draws out even latent as well as actual pain, brings it to a head, and then it dies and disappears completely. This is one of the laws by which it operates.

Now there was no room for doubt that the Lord

had given me the power of healing or, more correctly had developed in me a capacity to receive and transmit the Power.

I must, however, clearly state, at this place in my account of the Ministry, that the Healing Power is God's Power. It is not a power the person who ministers possesses. He merely receives and transmits it to the needy one. " Ye shall receive power when that the Holy Ghost is come upon you," said Jesus. It is a power that is imparted, controlled and applied by the Holy Ghost, and also withdrawn by Him when the patient has had enough of it for the time being, or for the particular part of the body being treated. The capacity to be the transmitting instrument is developed by a continuous process of surrender, cleansing and sanctification by the Holy Spirit and a regular practice of the consciousness of the Divine Presence. It is not strictly a gift we receive and possess, but rather a capacity which, under God, we develop.

After that first service the time had come to think out my plan of action and I decided to follow strictly the example of Jesus Christ in His Healing work.

The first thing that struck me about His Healing Ministry was, that He did not conduct specially advertised and organised public services. He ministered healing to the people whenever and wherever they or their friends appealed to Him. He was always ready to go to their homes if the patient was not at hand. " I will come and heal him," was the immediate reply to the Centurion, when he appealed on behalf of his suffering servant. Up to that time, Jesus seems to have felt it necessary to be actually present with the sufferer before He could heal him. It would almost appear as if the Centurion's request : " Speak the word only and my servant shall be healed ", was the first occasion when it occurred to Jesus that He could heal at a distance. There may have been an element of amazement in the way he reacted to the man's faith. Matthew tells us, that He marvelled and said : " Verily I say unto you, I have not found so great faith, no, not in Israel." Was it a greater faith than He had Himself? Luke verifies the story in its essential features.

Healing through public services specially organised and advertised was, in view of the scriptural guidance I had chosen, out of the question. So I went to those homes in my congregation where the need was greatest. The first case was a lady who had been ten years in bed suffering from rheumatoid arthritis. After the first services her pain disappeared almost immediately, but it took three months of weekly services before she was able to stand and walk around her room.

My second case was a cancer sufferer, an old lady whose son asked if I would visit her. She had been in an infirmary to have an operation for the disease. The surgeon had told the family that the trouble was too far advanced and she was being sent home to die, probably in a matter of weeks. The son did not know I had started the Healing Ministry as I asked those to whom I ministered not to speak about it outside their family circle because I feared scoffers. He asked me to prepare his mother for death. I went and prayed with the dying woman and gave her the laying on of hands, above the blankets. The pain disappeared and in a few days she was able to leave bed and eat. She required repeated services and lived for a year in comparative comfort.

This was not my only cancer case. I shall discuss later a young man, sent home to die of a cancer diagnosed histologically, that had attacked all his organs, who to-day is normal in every way and still engaged in heavy work. An old lady sent home to die in a few weeks of this dreadful disease, which had affected her spine, still is alive after nine years. My experience, however, with cancer and other reputedly incurable diseases is that while there are cases of cure, or as the doctors term it, "apparent cure" they are isolated and few; but almost invariably the pain goes, the patient gets peace and comfort after healing services and life is lengthened, sometimes by months, sometimes by years.

Something is imparted by this Ministry of prayer plus the laying on of hands that prayer alone cannot impart. This is a vivid experience of the peace that Jesus bequeathed for the benefit of all mankind, it affects the whole personality, body, mind and spirit. Not only does this peace fill the patient's soul. Members of his family who are present during the service also benefit. Indeed, usually they feel they too have a "healing" as well as the patient. I give the following instance to show that even where a cure is not effected and death ensues, such help and comfort and peace are imparted to the dying that their families are ever grateful.

Janet, as I shall call her, was a bright, charming and beautiful girl of fifteen, but she had developed abdominal cancer and, like many more, was sent home to die. The time came when, her doctor's sedation losing its effect, she began to suffer intensely. Her mother asked if I would help and with the first service the pain completely disappeared. An important difference, it is worthy of noting, between relief from the pain which the Divine Healing Power gives and medical sedation is that the Divine Power does not confuse the patient's mind, nor render him unconscious. It enables him to sleep, but the sleep is natural. In order to keep Janet free from pain I had to give her a service every day for some weeks until she peacefully died. This happened a few years ago and ever since her mother, out of gratitude for the help given to her daughter, takes out her car every Thursday to bring to my clinic a young lady suffering from multiple sclerosis and who would otherwise be unable to attend.

A similar case of gratitude which verifies the reality of a complete cure is that of a maiden lady who lives alone in a little house some seven miles from Glasgow. When in good health she was a great church worker and revelled in every form of Christian service that would help others. She also loved gardening.

But that insidious disease osteo-arthritis laid hold upon her and gradually its ruthless onslaught made her give up all the work she enjoyed—even housework. For twelve years she scarcely was able to walk. Every possible form of medical treatment was applied in vain. Finally, and I have no doubt, in hopeful despair, she was brought to my clinic.

I gave her weekly services for three months before the pain began to lessen. She had faith and patience and she persisted in coming. Within one year her suffering was greatly relieved; within two she was completely cured.

To show her gratitude and to prove the reality of her cure, every Thursday she travels by bus from her home into the Gorbals of Glasgow bringing flowers and fruit to lonely widows and maiden ladies. To do so she climbs, sometimes, fourteen four-flight stairs—and in the Gorbals stairs are steep and floors high—in one afternoon. She has been doing this for four years.

When my friend finishes this wonderfully charitable task she comes to my clinic for a service, not that she needs one, but just because she finds, like many others, that services are the most effective tonic available. They renew and revitalise the whole person as no other tonic can.

When, I should say, that lady first came to my clinic I told her to ask her doctor's permission to continue and to tell him what we do there. She replied that she was not going near her doctor until she was cured and she kept to her resolution. When cured she visited the doctor, let him see what had been accomplished and told him how it had happened.

His comment was, " Do you remember that seven years ago I had your tonsils taken out?"

" Yes," she replied, " I remember that."

" Well," returned the doctor, " that is what has cured you."

I have a theory that this Divine Healing Power does three things. First it enables the patient to derive more benefit from the doctor's treatment than would otherwise happen.

Second it helps to set the natural healing powers of the body in operation.

Third, if anything more is required then the Divine Power is capable of supplying whatever may be needed. As Jesus said : " With God all things are possible." But from the claim this doctor made I wonder if it may not be that this Divine Power also enables a patient to derive delayed benefit from medical treatment, even after seven years—like a post-dated cheque.

My experience with rheumatic cases is that every type yields, but it requires time and patience. Rheumatoid arthritis, fibrositis, sciatica and lumbago respond fairly quickly but osteo-arthritis and neuritis are very stubborn. Two to four months pass before the pain and restrictive movement in osteo-arthritis begin to disappear. The removal of the dense encrustation around the affected joint and the consequent immobility is a gradual process. Weekly services are required. Some sufferers come expecting us to perform instantaneous cures as Jesus did, and they lose patience and give up hope when cure is delayed. But with faith and patience, especially patience, every rheumatic condition yields.

When I use the term "cure", I should explain that I mean the patient is sufficiently restored to health to resume a normal working life. Medical opinion might not recognise such cases as real cures but only temporary remissions. In fact I am tempted to think that medical opinion does not believe anyone is completely cured until the patient is dead, the apparent cure being only a matter of remission.

I find it interesting to speculate on what happened in after-life to those whom Jesus cured. Were his cures permanent or only temporary? We feel we must believe the former, but since we have no after-history of any of them we do not know. We know only that those whom even He healed are now dead.

In cases of serious illness I have always insisted on the patient telling his doctor what is being done at the Healing Service and securing his permission before

giving a service. Only in one case has a doctor refused to co-operate. But as most of the people who
ask for this form of treatment have been told by their
doctors, " I can do nothing more for you, it now rests
entirely between yourself and God ", many do not
think it necessary to inform their Medical Advisers.
But I always advise them to continue—if possible—
medical treatment. This means that in every case of
cure or partial cure, the doctor has at least a share of
the credit. It is a mistake, I believe, for those of us
who exercise this Ministry of Divine Healing to over-
state our claims and boast that we alone did it. It
makes the healing no less divine when we give a doctor
his fair share of credit.

CHAPTER 5

HEALING THE UNBELIEVER

A young business man was sent home from an infirmary to die of lung cancer; he had only a few weeks to live, according to the infirmary authorities. His family doctor was asked to keep him free of pain and his relatives asked the doctor to agree to my giving healing services to the sick man. The doctor was delighted to let me do what I could and said he would keep a close watch on the results. With the first service the patient's pain stopped—in a few days he was back at work. But I had to give frequent services to keep the pain away.

Shortly after the first day the doctor called to see how the patient fared in the morning before going to business. After a chat the man set off and the doctor, watching him from a window walking smartly down the street, said to his sister : " Well, there certainly must be something in Mr. Peddie's service which is beyond our power and knowledge."

The young man went on like this for about a year, then suddenly collapsed and died a few days later. The services had given him an extra year of life, mostly devoted to his usual business.

One of the objections I have heard a learned professor raise against the Healing Ministry is that those who exercise it have neither the medical knowledge nor the experience to enable them to diagnose any case and this in his view, was essential to healing. But all the cases that come to us or are brought, or to whom we are asked to go, have been thoroughly examined and tested by their own doctors and by specialists in hospitals and infirmaries before our help is sought.

The sick are always able to inform us, even in technical terms, of the medical opinions of their conditions. For example, a minister in Dundee wrote asking if I would help one of his members who was suffering from a distressing chest condition. I replied saying that if his friend would come to my clinic I would do what I could for him. I have before me as I write a letter from the man himself in which he describes his trouble according to what medical authorities have told him. Here are his words.

"I have been to various hospitals, both in Scotland and the South of England and the answer they gave me was to take things easy and retire from work. The tubes inside the lungs are over-stretched and so there is no elasticity which means all the air in and out of the lungs must be forced and this leads to bouts of extreme breathlessness and a tensioning of the muscles, it also affects the nerves. This condition produces breathlessness and is known as Bronchiectasis with emphysema."

This is the sort of thing we get from all patients except those who tell us the doctors are baffled and cannot discover what is the matter with them. The fact of the matter is that the Holy Spirit is the one and only complete and unerring diagnostician and healer and we leave both the diagnosing and the healing entirely in His hands.

We require more time to impart and maintain benefit, not to speak of effecting a complete cure, because we are inferior to Jesus Christ in surrender, purity, sanctification, and in our sense of unity with God. A consequence of our inferiority is that God has to make up in time what we lack in spiritual qualifications. If Jesus Christ were here, every case, even the most difficult, would be instantaneously and completely cured, as we learn from the Bible. We do however have occasional instantaneous results.

One night when I returned home at 10.30, after giving healing services, I found a message to inform me that one of my members, a young married man, wished me to call no matter how late. For a whole week, the message said, he had been suffering intolerable pain from a carbuncle and the doctor had given him penicillin to which he was allergic. He had suffered days and nights of sickness as well as pain and could stand it no longer. When I arrived the man looked terribly ill. After the usual brief prayer I laid my hands on his head and in a few seconds his pain, though at the other end of his body, was completely gone; and so was his sickness. I then laid a hand on his clothes at the point adjacent to the carbuncle, and left it there until the healing power, which expressed itself in intense heat felt by the patient, was withdrawn by the Holy Spirit.

This was to ensure that the pain was completely gone and in the hope that it would not return. That man was at church the following Sunday. The sickness had not returned but there was a slight pain and I gave him a service of a few minutes. Again the pain disappeared instantaneously. The patient was starting a new job the following day. His doctor had written him off as cured after the first healing.

Most doctors now have agreed that with this ministry something happens at the intellectual and spiritual level but not at the physical level, although, in recent years, psychosomatic conditions have been recognised by the profession. Certainly the first effect of a service is to heighten the level of the mind and spirit. There comes to the patients immediately after the laying on of hands, a sense of soothing and comfort and a strange peace as if all the burdens and cares of life were removed. " Oh, this is wonderful. How lovely," are the usual comments made. This condition is the work of the Holy Spirit, and there is no doubt that the spiritual power can produce physical results also. Spirit can influence matter. If it cannot then there could have been no such thing as Creation. God, a spiritual being, created the original substance from which this material universe has evolved. But quite apart from the psychological effect we have physical results from this ministry.

Hands twisted and deformed by rheumatic conditions became normal. Locked joints are loosened. Corns and bunions disappear as the following experience demonstrated. A minister's wife was suffering agony from a corn and asked if I could do something for her. After holding her foot in my hands for a few minutes, the pain went from it. Three days afterwards she looked at the foot, touched it and found that the corn was loose. She lifted out the core and still there was no pain. Some time previously I had discovered, one might say by chance, that corns respond to this power.

When on my visiting routine one night I called on a lady who was in bed suffering from asthma. She lived alone but a friend was spending the evening with her. This was in the early days of my healing and neither had heard of the work. I talked to them of the Healing Ministry of Jesus and the commission He gave His disciples and us; I said to the suffering one that if she wished I would give her a healing service and she assured me she would be grateful. Ten minutes afterwards she felt completely cured and said she would return to work next day.

When the visitor saw this she said : " Mr. Peddie, I have a very painful corn on my left foot, can you do anything about that?" In the circumstances I could not refuse so I said, " Of course I can," and took her foot in my hands. In a few minutes she had complete relief.

" Oh, Mr. Peddie," she then said, " I have a very sore bunion on my other foot. Would you help it too?"

Again I did as she wished with the same result. Next day that woman went to work without pain, and whereas formerly she had to wear soft slippers she could now go through the whole day's task wearing ordinary leather shoes. That is some ten years ago and she has had neither corn nor bunion since.

A lady who had been a nursing sister in hospitals for sixteen years before her illness was an even more striking example. She had suffered from trigeminal neuralgia on the right side of her face and after surgical treatment while the pain disappeared the right half of her head was completely numb. I gave her three services and when she came for the fourth she told me that feeling had come back to her face and she was grateful.

" But," I said, " doctors claim this healing ministry cannot produce physical results."

" Well," she replied, " if your services have reconstituted the nerves of my face, as they have done, and

I know what I'm speaking about, then something *has* happened at the physical level."

One Christmas Eve a young married man asked me if I would go and minister to his wife. She was expecting a baby due to be born in May and she had developed an intense pain in her back and right leg. The medical department of the infirmary she attended had failed to diagnose the source of her pain and sent her to the surgical department where a surgeon told her she had a slipped disc in the lumbar region. It was of a difficult type and would require an operation but as the woman was pregnant the surgeon told her he could not operate until the baby was born. She would just have to go home and lie for five months on a rigid bed and endure the pain as best she could; even sedation might injure the baby.

After a few days of following this counsel to the letter her family doctor stepped in and told her she simply could not lie on a rigid bed for five months. She must get up occasionally and sit on a rigid chair with the affected leg on a rigid stool at the same level. I called at the house and found her sitting on this chair and stool. After the usual prayer I laid my hands briefly on her head, which calmed her mind and soothed her nerves. Then I placed a hand on her back at the point of trouble and the other hand opposite it, neither hand exercising any pressure. I asked her to sway gently from side to side and then up and down six times each, pivoting on my hands but stopping as soon as she felt the pain increasing. One turn of this and the pain was gone from the spine but not the leg. A little further treatment and the leg was well. The young wife got up from the chair and took a few steps, still in comfort. She began to dance and still she moved without pain. Then like Peter's wife's mother in the Bible story she wanted to minister to me by making a cup of tea but I had no time to wait for tea so she came to the door to see me off.

Next morning that young mother left home to do her shopping and her doctor, happening to pass along the street in his car, saw her and was so astounded, he had to stop and ask what had happened. The following week she reported to the maternity clinic and when she entered the resident doctor asked in amazement: " What's happened to you. Who did this?" She told him and he studied her record, drummed with his pencil on the table, and finally remarked : " Well, there must be something in it after all."

I have given enough evidence to show, I hope, that the healing ministry has pronounced results at the physical level. I will add that in the course of my clinical work I have given services to two ladies crippled by slipped discs in the upper spine, each wearing a large stiff collar provided by the infirmaries to give a measure of ease and comfort. Each left my clinic, the one smiling with the collar under her arm, the other laughing with her collar stuffed into a large handbag.

At the beginning of the revival of the healing ministry in Scotland, especially when it became a public issue, the medical profession became interested almost to the point of alarm. The first reaction was one of scepticism. Committees were formed to investigate the movement and individual doctors and professors selected test cases to be ministered to under medical supervision. Every opportunity and encouragement was given to the minister concerned to prove the worth of the ministry. The consensus of medical mind was that while exceptional mental and spiritual benefit could not be denied, there was no conclusive proof of physical improvement due to the services.

The explanation however may be that you cannot put the Holy Ghost into a test tube. Also under test conditions the personality of the servant of God ministering may not be properly adjusted.

Church committees at various levels have also been called in to investigate, encourage and guide this movement along sane and safe channels, and they have done their work most conscientiously. But it is to be feared that to thinking men and women the very appointment of such committees merely serves to expose the poverty of the Church's faith and proves that officially the Church of Christ is not sure that its great Founder and Master spoke the truth or that His commandment "Heal the sick" is to be taken seriously.

A further aspect of the physical effects of the ministry may be seen in the following incident. A doctor friend came to one of my services bringing instruments to check my blood pressure as I prayed over the patient, who happened to be my wife Netta. There was little wrong with my wife but a service always had a tonic effect on her. My friend took my blood pressure before the service and to his surprise found it to be 110. Several times he tested to make sure no mistake had been made. According to medical reckoning my pressure should have been in the region of 170 : at 110 it was, to him, incredible that my legs could carry me. Before the service he also took Netta's pressure and found it normal. After the service, which lasted only five minutes, he took our pressures again, and while mine had gone up by 20 degrees to 130, Netta's had come down by ten degrees.

I grant that the same effects can be produced by orthodox medical means, yet that does not alter the fact that the Divine Healing Power produces such physical phenomena. When I gave that healing service to my wife I had no thought in my mind of ministering to myself. It was the Healing Grace of God passing through me to her that produced these physical effects.

Always I am vividly conscious of the wonderful form of Divine Energy passing through me when giving services. I know it is the degree of spiritual sensitivity which I have developed through my regular and disciplined practice of the consciousness of the Divine Presence, that makes me aware of it. It may also be that every time I give a service the same benefit is imparted to myself; and this would explain why giving a service of Divine Healing does not exhaust but rather reinvigorates one.

I may add that doctors need have no fear that the time may come when their patients will have more faith in us than in them. Alas, in the eyes of many, even in the Church, we still are witchdoctors, to be approached cautiously and only when in despair. Such indeed is the measure of the Christian faith of many —both in the pulpit and the pew.

What is the place and function of faith in the Healing Ministry? I need not attempt to define faith here. It probably has different meaning for different minds. Stauffer, the great modern theologian, finds different definitions for it even in Bible characters. He says that for Jesus faith was " an audacious assertion of a possibility ", and for Paul and John " an abasement before the Glory of God ". For the author of the Epistle of the Hebrews " evidence of the invisible " and to the author of Revelations " the fidelity of the martyr ". As I dare not enter into controversy with such great minds, I merely will say that for me the highest type and degree of faith is a vivid sense of co-operation with God.

That is certainly what it should and does mean for all who exercise this ministry effectively. Here I would add that there is no power in faith in itself (*per se*). All the power associated with faith lies in God's response to it. It is true that Jesus said to several whom He healed " Thy faith has made thee whole ", but by this He meant " thy faith has made it possible for God to heal you, without your faith He could not have done it ". The power is entirely of God. Hence it is not strictly correct to call this ministry faith healing as some do.

Many humble and good folk feel that they have not enough faith to receive benefit from the ministry, but I cannot write too emphatically that they need have no such fear. While faith at its highest and best is essential in the one who ministers, and while patients who have great and simple faith are more responsive and easier to heal, those who have no faith in God, or in this form of ministry, can most surprisingly be healed. It seemed as if, in His infinite compassion, He cannot resist their need. He cannot resist even the crude unbeliever.

In the year I started this work my family and I spent some months in our country home and Netta and I had occasion one afternoon to call at a farm.

When we arrived the farmer's wife told us her husband had been seized with an attack of lumbago. He was in his bedroom suffering great agony and she asked me to visit him. The woman did not know I had started healing work. When I reached the bedroom the farmer scarcely was able to speak, not to think of moving, with pain. He was by no means a fervent Christian and when, after chatting in a friendly way for some time I asked: "Would you like me to have a word of prayer with you?" he answered, "What the hell good would that do?" I just laughed, and thought: "here is a man who at least is sincere. He says what he means and means what he says." There was something good in him that could be tapped if I chose the right approach.

So in my mind I asked the Father to guide me and while waiting for His response, I talked awhile in friendly conversation, one-sided for it was painful for the man even to speak.

In a little time I was led to say: "I want to tell you that there is a strange kind of electricity in my hands and when I put them on people who are suffering, the pain usually goes."

Turning half round and placing a hand on his lumbar region he said: "Then, for God's sake, clap them on there."

I "clapped" them on "there" and in a few minutes he said: "Man, that's awfa queer. That's funny a' the pain is gethering to a pint aneath yir hand. There mun be an awfa power in those hands of yours. The doctor left some ointment there on the mantelpiece. Tak' some o' that ointment and rub it on they hands o' yours and I'll be better."

I did not use the ointment but left my hands on his

back and in ten minutes all his pain was gone. The farmer sat up in bed and, looking at me, said :

" There mun be an awfa electricity in your body. Does a watch gang on you?"

I replied : " This is not electricity. This is the power that Jesus promised when He said ' Ye shall receive power after that the Holy Ghost is come upon you and ye shall be witnesses unto me '." I continued : " Jesus told us to preach the gospel and heal the sick. I have been preaching the Gospel to the best of my ability for over thirty years but not many really believe it."

" My God," he replied, " they'll believe this."

That farmer struck the real purpose of this ministry. It is to get people really to believe and to put an edge on their faith. Next day he was out of bed and at work as usual. The service had brought him nearer God than ever he had been in his life.

This is not an isolated case. There was James, a rigger on the Clyde who was a Communist. He had no use for God or the Bible. James developed rheumatics and a chest and heart condition. Gradually his disabilities increased. The doctor pronounced him seriously ill and said that even if he recovered he never again would be able to work. James' wife, a staunch church-woman, did not tell me he was ill, so far was she from asking me to visit him because she knew a minister was the last man her husband would want to see. However when the doctor said he had only eight or nine weeks to live she thought it time to call in the minister, whether James wanted to see him or not. So I went. The poor soul was a pitiful sight, sitting on a chair because he was too far gone in pain to lie in bed. His heart and chest condition had intensified; his breathing was laboured; he scarcely could move his arms. After some preliminary conversation, I asked if he believed in God. He said nothing but gave me a queer look with his large eyes and turned away his head. I asked if he believed the Bible and his response was the same.

Then I said: " James, I know there is a God who cares for us all and I also know the Bible is true. Now James, Jesus said: 'These signs shall follow them that believe— they shall lay their hands on the sick and they shall recover '."

I then told him about the services with the laying on of hands which I was giving. Neither James nor his wife had heard of the Healing Ministry; the wife had called me to prepare him for death. I offered to give him a service if he was willing to receive it.

" Yes," he said, he was willing.

The service lasted about half an hour, after which James rose from his chair and his breathing was easier. He stood still for a few moments then raised his arms above his head and walked round the room. Halting he stretched the arms in all directions as if doing physical jerks and said in a loud clear voice :

" My God the Bible is true after all "

James received other services and in three months was back at work, continuing at it several years until he retired. He was grateful to God and did not keep his cure secret in the beginning, but calling on him one day as his minister, I asked :

" James do you ever speak to your mates about what cured you of that illness?"

" Oh, yes," he replied, " I gave my testimony for

the Lord and told them all about it, but when they began to laugh at me and pointing to their heads and saying I was mental, I stopped."

I think enough has been said to verify my statement that while great faith is essential in the person who ministers, it does not seem to be absolutely necessary in the recipient. I believe, however, that where faith abounds in the patient, a greater power abounds.

There are those too who while not actively opposed to God and religion are luke-warm in their attitude to Jesus. One might say that in their hearts they believe but in their lives they serve even less than half-heartedly. I had such a case and it had startling results.

Angus, who lived with his mother, was a decent hard-working fellow but did not attend church which worried the other member of the household. He took ill and was admitted to hospital for surgery but the operation was delayed because his temperature kept fluctuating. Many weeks passed and it began to look as if he would never be in a condition that would make it safe for the surgeon to go to work. At last, one evening, his distraught mother came to me and begged for assistance. I went to see Angus on a Friday and gave him a service. On Saturday, I called again and found his temperature normal. The following Monday the operation took place revealing, it seemed, a tragic condition, for the surgeon told the mother that Angus was suffering from cancer which had penetrated many of his organs. The poor man had two months to live, no more. They sent him home and his distraught mother prepared for the end. Angus did not know his fate but feeling terribly weak asked for me. I called on him twice during succeeding weeks and each time gave him a service. Then I ran into a very busy period of work when I literally had no time to give the man who, I had been told, was dying. I plunged into my tasks and, I confess, forgot him. Some months passed and then one evening my telephone rang and I answered. It was Angus and I felt crestfallen because one never can give enough attention to those who suffer. Without waiting for him to explain the reason for his call I burst into apologies and was floored by the answer.

"Oh, don't worry, Mr. Peddie. I know you're busy with sick people. But I thought you'd like to know I'm going back to work on Monday."

I did not know what to say but, indeed, I need have said nothing for Angus had not finished. He continued.

"I want you to do something else for me, Mr. Peddie. You see I'm getting married in two months. Will you marry me and Annie?"

I married the couple and they have lived happily ever since. This incident occurred many years ago and from time to time I still see Angus. He has done well at his job, has many interests outside his work and they centre on his home and his church for he has become an enthusiastic church-worker in his denomination.

I could relate other instances of unbelievers and half-believers being blessed in body, mind and spirit through these services.

Another question that arises is how far is it necessary to prepare the patient for the reception of service? Where time and opportunity are available one would naturally think that the more preparation the better results.

We hear of weeks of services of special preparation for intending recipients being held in churches before the arrival of some servant of God who heals in public.

This cannot be without avail, but all who exercise this ministry, whether in public or in private, must not forget that before any service can impart blessing the most important preparation is that of the ministering servant of God. Unless he is regularly and in some disciplined way preparing himself, or rather submitting himself to that thorough preparation which only the Holy Spirit can impart, the best results will not be obtained.

Where services are given to individuals privately, or with only some members of the family or a friend present, it always is necessary to have a confidential talk, allowing the needy one to unfold himself and unburden his mind. It may be necessary to ask some questions relative to the trouble involved and the diagnosis given by the doctor. The whole history of the case generally will flow forth in great volume, usually with the use of modern technical terms. Then it is wise to make clear to the suppliant the nature of the power that is to be applied, the source of that power, the impressions and sensations that may arise in the conscious mind during the service, and above all that such a service is in accord with the teaching, example and command of Our Lord Jesus Christ.

While this is going on the ministering one must be actuated by the thought and deep conviction that in spite of all he may say or do, unless the Holy Spirit uses what he says and does to prepare the suffering mind for the service, no adequate preparation will have been made.

Only Our Lord through His Holy Spirit can prepare anyone for such a service, but I must add that where sincerity of need and intention abound, He never fails to respond.

From the example of Jesus on the question of a patient's preparation, it would appear that very little is required. The only preparation He gave his patients was to ask the question : " Do you believe I can heal you?" The intensity of the power of the Holy Spirit operating through Him was such as to render extensive and prolonged preparation of the patient unnecessary.

A strange and thought-provoking, I believe, feature in the attitude of Our Lord to this question is that in His opinion, quite contrary to the opinion of His Church to-day, it is unnecessary to ask the patient to confess his sins and repent before giving a service of healing. Confession and repentance come after the service and the healing. This is because the service and the healing enable the patient to realise there is a God. Then it is that the unbeliever or doubter really begins to believe because he feels the power of God working mightily in him, just as the woman who touched the hem of Christ's garment felt the power affecting her, and, knowing she was healed, went boldly to Him and according to Mark told Him the truth. Was this not confession?

CHAPTER 6

OIL FROM GOD

Sin is due to unbelief. When a man truly believes he will not sin because his faith is sufficiently definite to enable the Holy Spirit to make it the intention of his soul not to sin. Confession and repentance follow after belief becomes operative as a result of the healing.

This became evident as the opinion of Jesus when He upbraided the cities wherein most of His mighty works were performed because they did not repent. "Woe unto thee Chorazin; woe unto thee Bethsaida; for if the mighty works which were done in you had been done in Tyre and Sidon they would have repented long ago in sackcloth and ashes." Note that Jesus said they would have repented *after* the mighty acts. My contention is verified by the explicit opinion of Jesus, and also, and more convincingly, by His practice. Never once did He make confession and repentance a condition of healing. Indeed, only twice does He mention sin throughout his crowded healing ministry.

These two solitary references were when He healed the man who was lowered through the roof and the cripple at the pool.

In the first case he anticipated the man's needless confession with an assurance of pardon. He said to him : " Son, thy sins be forgiven thee." This was the same as healing the man, as He pointed out to the complaining scribes.

74

It was the man's foolish belief that his sins could not be forgiven, that he had committed the unpardonable sin and this evidently was the cause of his physical affliction. When a man of Jesus' reputation assured him that this was not so, that he was needlessly worrying himself, he was released from the mental tension that was the root of his trouble. Here one might remark on the great number of men and women who come seeking healing and whose trouble mental and physical, is due to the same cause. Somehow they have come to believe they have committed the unpardonable sin. How strange it is that Jesus is reported to have believed in the reality of such a sin, a thought quite consistent with the hard, vengeful hearts of the Jewish religious leaders and teachers of that era but entirely alien to His mind. He not only came into the world to seek and save that which was lost but actually, according to the teaching of the Apostles and the belief of the Christian Church, went down into Hell to save the damned who presumably had committed the " unforgivable sin ". It is reasonable, he showed us, to believe that every sin sincerely repented is forgiven.

The man at the pool was a different proposition from the man let down through the roof. He was suffering because of his sins yet Jesus did not refer to those sins before healing him. He simply asked the poor fellow if he really wanted to be healed, and, finding him sincere in his desire, healed him. There was no demand that he should confess and repent, simply a kindly question : " Will thou be made whole?" But later Jesus found him in the temple and he was there because having experienced the reality of God and His Power and so really believing, he now repented and wished to confess. Did he confess to Jesus? I am sure he did and that Jesus in love and sympathy listened, comforted and guided but parted from him with the final warning : " Sin no more lest a worst thing come unto thee."

Such were the two only cases in Christ's healing ministry in which He makes reference to the sins of the patient, and in no case does He demand confession and repentance prior to the healing.

Why do we lay on hands? Chiefly because it was Jesus' usual method, so much so that when people asked for healing their words of request very often were : " Come and lay your hands upon him or her." Jairus made his appeal in these words : " My little daughter lieth at the point of death. I pray thee come and lay Thy hands on her that she may be healed and she shall live." (Mark 5, v. 23). We also read in Mark 8, v. 22, that at Bethsaida : " They bring a blind man unto Him and besought Him to touch him." The public evidently had the impression that He healed by laying on His hands. The reverse was also the case for many came eager to touch Him.

The woman with the hæmorrhage said : " If I may but touch His garment I shall be whole " (Matthew 9, v. 21). In Matthew 14, v. 35, we read that when " He was in Gennesaret the men sent out into all that country round about and brought unto Him all that were diseased and besought Him that they might only touch the hem of His garment." In Mark 3, v. 10, we find a whole multitude pressing upon Him " for to touch Him." Mark indicates the universality of this opinion of His healing power and the method by which it was imparted when He tells us that : " Whither so ever He entered into villages or cities or country they laid the sick in the streets and besought Him that they might touch if it were but the border of His garment " (Mark 6, v. 56).

It is evident therefore that while Jesus could heal by His mere word, He seems to have resorted chiefly to the laying on of hands. The reason probably was that while the Divine Healing Grace could be communicated by means of speech and thought, it was more effective on direct contact. His hands were the readiest and most convenient means of achieving this. They were instruments of the Holy Spirit, created, moulded and shaped for the purpose of manipulating and imparting spiritual power and only secondarily for dealing with material things exercising physical force. The same may be true of our hands and I believe it is so. I have evidence that greater benefit is imparted by the laying on of even our human hands than through prayer alone, as the following case, one of many, suggests.

The father of the chaplain at one of our universities was dying and the son asked me to try and help him. I gave the old gentleman weekly services from which he derived comfort and peace and a sense of real help. While I was doing this his own minister expressed a wish to be present at one of the services and arrived at the time arranged. But I was prevented from going on the appointed night and could not notify the family. The minister waited till it was evident I was not coming and, feeling it his duty to take my place, he engaged in prayer with the sufferer but did not lay on hands.

When the prayer ended the patient thanked him and said : " That was very helpful and comforting but it was nothing like the relief and comfort that Mr.

Peddie's services give." The difference was entirely
due to the laying on of hands and not to any special
virtue which the other minister lacked. Had he had
sufficient faith in himself to lay on hands, as an
instrument of God, the result would have been the
same as in my case, perhaps better.

Now Jesus knew, as by His Grace He has led us to
discover, that the healing power of which He was a
perfect instrument was not mere magic but Divine
Grace or energy which is not arbitrary nor chaotic in
its behaviour but operates according to definite divine
decrees which are spiritual laws. One of these is that
in most cases prayer plus the laying on of hands
imparts a greater and richer flow of divine healing
grace than can be achieved by prayer alone. Hence
it is that we find Jesus laying on hands much more
often than not. On searching the Scriptures with this
question in view one almost is led to conclude that He
adopted the method of actual physical contact in cases
where the trouble had a physical basis and healing by
His mere word in cases where the trouble was essen-
tially mental or spiritual.

Be that as it may, it is clear from the Bible record
that He healed many more by His touch than by His
word to judge from the cases of which details are
given. It is impossible to reckon up the exact number
of either. We read in Luke 4, v. 40, " Now when the
sun was setting all they that had any sick with diverse
diseases, brought them unto Him and He laid His
hands on every one of them and healed them." He
healed multitudes and no description is given of the
method used. In Luke 12, v. 15, we read simply that
on one occasion, " Great multitudes followed Him and
He healed them all." He may have used His hands

on that occasion too. Here I would emphasise the fact that the reason we lay on hands is that through them definite substantial healing power is conveyed by the Holy Spirit.

I once heard a minister (now a professor) say during a lecture on Divine Healing that the touch of Jesus in healing was merely a touch of sympathy. It had just the same purpose and effect which we all have when we lay our hands sympathetically on someone in trouble. Nothing, in my belief, could be further from the truth. Only on one occasion was the touch of Jesus a touch apparently of mere sympathy. That was when the tremendous experience of the transfiguration had left Peter, James and John limp and prostrate with fear.

There we read that " Jesus came and touched them and said arise and be not afraid." It would be quite legitimate to interpret that touch as indicating only sympathy but since Jesus must have touched each separately it also is reasonable to conclude that power also passed through His hands, gave substantial expression to His sympathy and had revitalising and tonic effects. It is surely a shallow scholarship that can reduce the actions of Our Lord to a mere human level; it indicates, I suggest, a gross ignorance of spiritual reality and the powers of the world to come. No wonder Jesus said : " Father I thank thee that thou hast hid these things from the wise and the prudent and hast revealed them unto babes " (Matthew 11, v. 25).

The Healing Grace of God not only passed through the hands of Jesus to the afflicted one; it radiated through His whole body. We read that " as many as touched Him were made perfectly whole " (Matthew

14, v. 22). This also is a feature of the Healing Ministry of to-day and what is more it does not appear to be always necessary that there should be actual contact. It usually happens that when a service is being given in a home with members of the family present, some feel they too have received a healing although no hands were laid on them. Still more is it surprising when one devoted to this work enters a home with no intention of giving a service and no mention of sickness in the house, and some member of the household suffering from some complaint of which the visitor is quite ignorant, is healed or at least cured of pain.

In the early days of my Healing Ministry when few members of my congregation knew about it I called on an elderly couple in a friendly capacity. There was no talk of healing or pain or sickness. Both appeared to be in normal health and after we drank a cup of tea I proceeded on my round of visitation. That evening the husband had occasion to come to my vestry to get a paper signed and when he was leaving he turned to me and said : " Mr. Peddie, do you know what my wife said to me when you left our house this afternoon ?"

" No, I do not," I replied.

" Well," he answered, " she said to me Mr. Peddie brought a strange healing power into the house with him to-day. As soon as he came my sciatic pain began to leave me and by the time he left it was completely gone and he did not know I had pain."

Strange things happen in the exercise of this ministry. On another occasion I and my family were in the country having tea at the home of my wife's parents. It was quite a large family gathering and when the meal was over Grandma said : " I made John sit next to me because I had a very bad pain in my leg and I just knew that if he sat beside me the pain would go, and it has gone completely."

Now with Grandma the relief from the pain (of which I was quite ignorant) may have been purely psychological, but not in the case of the other old lady. The Healing Power does apparently radiate through the whole body and can affect others—even at some distance. That was why the prophet stretched himself three times on the dead child to revive him and also why Paul embraced Eutychus to restore him (Kings 17, v. 21; Acts 20, v. 9 and 10). I think Jesus was referring to this spiritual power when He said : " If any man thirst let him come unto Me and drink. He that believeth in Me out of his body shall flow rivers of living water." Even Jesus had to resort to material terms in order to express the spiritual truth and convey the spiritual power which He embodied and unveiled to mankind.

Always it must be remembered that in the early apostolic age the Holy Ghost was communicated by the laying on of hands. Apart from Jesus Christ only on one occasion is the Holy Ghost reported to have come upon the people through preaching. That was when Peter was speaking in the house of Cornelius. When Paul laid his hands on converts at Ephesus the Holy Ghost came upon them. The same happened at Samaria to Philip's converts when Peter and John laid hands on them. Again Ananias laid hands on Paul " that he might be filled with the Holy Ghost ".

It is to be regretted that the Church seems to have lost this power. It ought to manifest itself when hands are laid on young ministers at the ordination service.

I am sure it is the intention of God that the ordained should not merely be set apart to preach and administer the sacraments, but should also be endowed by the Holy Ghost with power to heal as well as preach.

In connection with the laying on of hands there arises the question of anointing with oil. I always took it for granted that the oil referred to in healing was some form of man-made oil such as olive oil. I never would have dreamed of thinking otherwise. But the Lord had something else to tell me on this question and He told me in a most convincing manner. It happened when I was giving a service to a brother minister and my hands were on his brow and face. Suddenly he said to me: " Peddie, your hands are oily. You are anointing me with oil." I lifted my hands; we both looked at them. All over them there was a film of oil with solitary globules here and there. It was no illusion; it was a physical reality. I continued to minister to my friend and in a little while he said: " Peddie, the oil is perfumed." And so it was. It had a strange sweet pleasant aroma.

As time went on similar experiences of this oil recurred. On one occasion a brother minister asked me to go with him to a hospital to give a service to a young lad who, according to medical opinion, had only some three weeks to live. The boy was a victim of tuberculous peritonitis. After a brief prayer we laid our hands on his head following this up by drawing our hands slowly and lightly over his whole body above the bedclothes. From the moment that service began the lad felt he was being healed and he was out of hospital in a matter of weeks. To-day he is a strong vigorous active young man able for a heavy day's work. And when he speaks of his illness and its cure, he tells of the strange experience he had when we laid hands on him. He declares he was anointed with oil from head to foot.

Other cases have verified the reality of this feature of the ministry and it is not explained by saying that the hands begin to sweat, as one member of a committee investigating the matter suggested. The oil appears only for a minute or two when and where required and then suddenly disappears. Sometimes it appears on one hand only while the other remains normal.

As a result of experience I have come to the conclusion that the oil is a precipitate from God's own substance through the alembic of a surrendered personality in exactly the same way as the original substance from which the material universe was evolved was a precipitate from God through the alembic of the personality of the Son. "All things were made by Him and without Him was not anything made that was made " (John 1, v. 3).

We are told in Mark 6, v. 13, that the disciples anointed with oil many that were sick and healed them. I believe this was no man-made oil but oil direct from God. Why, I wonder, should it be considered impossible for the Almighty Creator to deposit oil as a precipitate from his own substance on the hands of consecrated men when we know nowadays that mere man, himself, as a scientist, can project on a screen on this earth, pictures that originate on the moon? Surely it is folly to deny God a greater genius than man, His mere creature, possesses and exercises to such effect.

Although there is no record in the Bible of Jesus using oil of any kind I believe the Holy Spirit used

Him also in this way. He never attempts to explain the forms and varieties of the Divine Healing Grace of which He was so perfect an instrument when in the flesh. His generation could not have understood Him as He was well aware, hence His silence and His explanation of that silence: " I have many things to say unto you but ye cannot bear them now " (John 16, v. 12). They could not understand or accept them then, but we of this generation, with our modern approach to a knowledge and understanding of the ultimate nature of matter, can both understand and accept what the Holy Spirit is revealing to-day of what He then left unsaid.

Further, I believe, the oil referred to in James 5, v. 14, was of this same nature, a precipitate from God. If it was man-made oil then that argues for a late date for the epistle at a time when the Church's faith had gone blunt and had lost its early spirituality.

There also is this to be said : if man-made oil had been used for healing by Divine Decree in New Testament days, then the kind of oil used would have been mentioned or a prescription for its composition would have been given as in the case of the anointing oil in Old Testament times. In Exodus 30, v. 23, we read : " Take thou also unto thee principal spices, of pure myrrh 500 shekels, and of sweet cinnamon half as much even 250 shekels, and of sweet calamus 250 shekels, of cassia 500 shekels, after the shekel of the sanctuary, and of oil olive an hin; and then thou shalt make it an oil of holy ointment, an ointment compound after the art of the apothecary. It shall be an holy anointing oil."

It is true that certain oils have healing power and also that oil used sacramentally may have healing effects at all levels, but I and those of my brethren who have had experience of it know that in this Ministry of Divine Healing God does precipitate oil from the invisible realm when and where necessary if a suitable instrument is available.

I now give extracts from a letter received from a lady in a Church of England Home in Yorkshire, who was present at a conference when I gave lectures on healing and referred to this mysterious oil. She verifies my words about the oil and also the spiritual blessing conveyed through this work.

" Perhaps you remember that when you were here you ministered to me for my eyesight. I am more than grateful to be able to tell you that they are already much better and I see ever so many things which I could not see before, especially out of doors. I know that the healing is now going on and I want to thank you and also to thank God for this. All the day after you had laid your hands on me I was aware of the scent of the oil. It was quite unmistakable and to be honest I had not believed it was true when you said it but there it was in my nostrils again and again. The following day it had gone. I shall always remember your visit as one of the most outstanding experiences I have ever known. It opened my spiritual eyes to great realities."

CHAPTER 7

GOD'S ALLY, THE DOCTOR

An objection raised against the Healing Ministry is that in removing pain it may cause danger to the patient. It is true that the services remove pain; there is no doubt about it. But as we are dealing with an expression of The Divine Power, controlled and directed by the Holy Spirit, there is a law that operates in cases where danger might arise from the removal of pain. In such cases the pain does not disappear or if it does, as soon as the healing hand is removed it returns. This means that either an operation is required or treatment only a hospital or infirmary can give. I discovered this from experience.

On the 14th of March, 1952, at 4 a.m. Richard, my son, sleeping in the same bedroom, asked me to give him a service of Divine Healing. For two hours he had been suffering intense pain in his abdomen. He declared apologetically, that he could stand it no longer and asked would I try to give him relief? After brief prayer I laid my hands on the affected part and in a few minutes the pain was gone. But no sooner had I removed my hands than it returned with equal severity. I replaced my hands on the same point, again the boy got relief, but on lifting my hands his agony was repeated.

This went on for thirty minutes or so. In spite of my utmost effort at surrender to the Power of God and conscious co-operation with Him, the pain kept returning every time I raised my hands.

At 4.30, I knew that here was something that had to be dealt with by doctor or surgeon. Medical attention was imperative and had I phoned a doctor it would have taken him some time to come, and he might have kept Richard at home for a day or two for diagnostic purposes.

I was sure no time should be lost so I called a taxi and delivered my son to an infirmary before 5 a.m. He was admitted and at 9 a.m., four hours later, was operated upon. At 11 a.m. I called to find out what had happened and the surgeon told me Richard's was one of the worst cases of peritonitis he ever had dealt with. He had done his best but could offer little hope of the boy's recovery. The prognosis was that if my son survived, he must remain in the infirmary for about three months, then spend six months in a convalescent home; and he never would be able to return to his profession as an engineer. Should he ever be able to work again, I was told, it could only be on very light tasks, and not in the city, but in the country. This was a severe shock to his mother and me—it happened so suddenly and without warning. It seemed our son would be a permanent invalid.

However, thanks to the wonderful work of that surgeon, the tender sympathy, care and efficiency of nurses, and the medical treatment he received, plus the healing services—chiefly absent healing I gave him —Richard was released from the infirmary ten days later. After three months' convalescence in a country annexe and a further three months in our house in the hills, he was able to resume his normal engineering tasks. During the next three years he travelled to work by motor bike, summer and winter, twenty miles there and twenty miles back; and in April 1957, he emigrated to Canada, where, in Toronto he still continues with the company that employed him in Scotland.

I have related this episode to demonstrate my contention that where it would be dangerous to remove pain by the ministry, the pain does not disappear or it returns when the hands are removed from the patient. It also shows how necessary it is for doctors, surgeons, nurses and ministers to co-operate.

To further illustrate my argument about pain and its removal I give another instance of a similar nature. One Saturday, around midnight, a weeping mother telephoned from the other side of Glasgow asking me to come to her son, a boy of twelve, who was in great pain.

She had phoned her doctor three times but he refused, at so late an hour, to come to the boy. Would I, she begged, try to give the child relief? I could not say no and in half an hour I was standing beside the boy. This, I saw at once, was not pretence or imagination in a petted spoiled only child, as the doctor had thought—I should say here that the doctor later told me that many a time he had been called at midnight to that same boy when nothing was wrong.

But on the night I called the poor lad truly was sick. The pain was in his right side, and, obviously symptomatic of appendicitis, it might require an operation. However, I gave my usual service, and when I put my hands on the sick boy the pain eased, then disappeared. I removed my hands, the pain returned and soon was as bad as ever. This process, the laying on of hands and release, the lifting of hands and the return of the pain, was repeated several times until

I was certain an operation was required, and immediately. So I called and asked for the doctor. On my call he came and diagnosed acute appendicitis. Immediately he summoned an ambulance and the boy was rushed to the infirmary where he was operated on, according to the surgeon, just in time.

A third example but with a different ending may confirm the existence of the law regarding pain and the ministry. This time it was a young girl to whom I was called. She was suffering from a fever condition, with discomfort and pain in throat and chest which, as usual, the service relieved and appeared to dissipate. Next day the pain returned. I thought at once of the law governing such cases. But the family doctor had diagnosed a disease that could not possibly need an operation; and was certain he and I together could effect a cure, so I said nothing about the possible need of an operation. Ultimately the girl had to be taken to hospital and there it was diagnosed that she had required an operation or treatment only a hospital could give—but it was too late.

Another objection raised against the ministry, especially in the medical world, is that it creates in a patient and his or her friends hopes that may not be realised. But, surely this charge can be brought against the medical profession, too. A doctor who does not inspire hope and confidence in his patient and the family concerned, and raise in their minds expectations of recovery, is lacking in the qualities essential to a doctor's personality. For a doctor, I suggest, to tell a patient that he can do no more for him is the same as giving him, while still alive, a death certificate.

" While there is life there is hope," is an adage that must endure and we who exercise this Ministry of Divine Healing do not intentionally act in a manner or say anything that might inspire bogus hope. We remind sufferers that we are not Jesus Christ and that they must not expect from us miracles such as He wrought. But, we say, we can promise peace of mind and a sense of comfort that nothing else can give.

CHAPTER 8

THE GREATEST PRIVILEGE

One of the most happy consequences of the movement is the revaluation of prayer as a dominant factor in the lives of people. Constant requests for prayer on behalf of the suffering are received by ministers. In most churches prayer groups have been organised to assemble regularly for the purpose of meeting the need. Great lists of suppliants are recorded in orderly fashion by these good folk and prayer is offered for each by name, usually the Christian name only being mentioned.

But it seems, rather strangely, that those who seek prayer for themselves or dear ones are foolishly ashamed to have their identity revealed and this shows to what a low level the prayer-life of the Church has fallen, how poor the appreciation of its work and how ungrateful to the Heavenly Father we all have become. By far the greatest privilege He has given us is the privilege to pray to Him.

" Let the redeemed say so," demands the Bible and this can be correctly translated " Let the healed say so." We may add : let those who seek healing say so, unafraid and unashamed, hiding nothing not even their full names. If they were to do this it might break down the barriers that obstruct the healing channels and enable the Divine Grace to flow forth in mightier volume.

But I must express a warning in connection with these prayer groups. There are dangers involved in such work against which we must be on our guard.

For one thing ministers must resist the temptation to refer their healing to auxiliary groups and neglect their duty to sweat in prayer and supplication for the needy and give private healing services in afflicted homes. In rendering this service to His own generation we are told that Jesus often had no time even to eat. Some ministers, I know, protest that their duty is to preach the Gospel and not to engage in healing work. But they would preach the Gospel far more effectively if they engaged in it; then they would give the Holy Spirit an opportunity to confirm the truth of their message. That is the true purpose of this work. It is the most effective evangelising agency at our disposal.

I remember a business man who came to my door one day and asked me to help him. He had been suffering for six years from a form of dermatitis that affected his head, hands and feet and he was in a sore plight. His physical appearance had been made hideous. Medical treatment (covering the six years) had relieved him only slightly; he had been in and out of hospitals many times but failed to get relief. I could not refuse him, especially because in the days of my gangster work this man had given me premises for one of my clubs. After three months of weekly services he was completely cured, could walk with comfort and was not ashamed of his head or hands. He continued to come for an occasional service just to make sure, I suppose, that the cure would be maintained. On one of these occasions he had no sooner entered the room where I gave these services than the doorbell rang. An A.A. man had arrived to ask for my membership fee of £2. As I did not have as much ready cash in the house I invited him in so I could

write a cheque. When my friend and patient saw me
about to do this he said :

" You are not going to write out a cheque for that
small amount, I'll pay it."

I protested, telling him I could not accept the
money, but my protests were in vain.

The A.A. man said : " It's a grand thing to have a
friend like this."

" Sir," said my friend, pointing at me, " this man
has shown me the way to Heaven."

No word of the healing, no thought of his cured
head, hands and feet, nothing but testimony of a
healed soul, such was the blessing the service had
bestowed on him. The memory of that blessing filled
his mind to the exclusion of all other benefits, even
the freedom to shake hands with people, the ability to
walk with comfort and the readiness to uncover his
head without shame. Only " this man has shown me
the way to Heaven ".

Another danger in connection with the establish-
ment of prayer groups is that those who pray may
come to regard themselves as mighty men and women
of prayer. This, indeed, might arise from much of the
teaching about prayer presently heard in our churches.

We hear it said that prayer is a mighty force; that
when we sincerely pray we generate energy that is
capable of achieving anything, that prayer is the
greatest power in the world, especially when actuated
by love. This is to misinterpret and misunderstand
the nature and laws of prayer. There is neither power
nor force nor energy of any kind in prayer by itself
per se.

All the power and virtue in prayer lies in God's
answer to our prayer. He alone must be given all

credit for anything that happens in response to prayers. We do not generate power of any kind when we pray. We simply make it possible for God to answer us.

To use material terms, as Jesus did when He spoke of bread and water to express the ultimate truth about Himself, I believe our prayers go to God in thought-waves and these are used by Him as carrier-waves over which He sends back responding waves of His love and grace. Our prayers are essential if we want God to do something special for ourselves or others, but their only function is that they facilitate God's response. Without our prayers the particularly needed blessing cannot come. Of course there are many kinds of prayer and blessings are poured out every day on unpraying men and women but we are not called upon to discuss these here. We only must let our whole prayer life be fraught with the spirit of humility and in beholding the results give God alone the credit and the glory.

Another aspect of the ministry is what we call Absent Healing.

All prayer for the sick who are not present at a service may be regarded as Absent Healing, but what we of the movement *mean* by the term is something quite different.

When we give Absent Healing we are doing something other than praying. The time for prayer has passed, our praying has ended and, as in direct heal-ing, we are co-operating with God in securing His answer. We go through exactly the same process as in direct healing. We are conscious of being charged with the Divine Power; we feel it passing through us to the sufferer and, like Jesus, we know that virtue is going out of us. In spirit we are present with the needy one; in imagination we can see the sick room in all its details. Sometimes it turns out that those details seen in imagination are exactly like the room, although the person giving the absent healing never has been there. More than that, the patient sometimes feels and sees the ministering one present.

Once I gave a service to an old man in his home. He was suffering from a chest condition and got considerable relief. Next day he was taken to an infirmary to undergo an operation. As soon as he arrived there his daughter called and asked me to give him Absent Healing from my sanctuary that night. I did so and next morning the sick man said to his nurse : " I'm ever so much better to-day. Mr. Peddie came to see me last night and gave me a service of Divine Healing and it has done me a lot of good. I am feeling fine now." Except in spirit, I had not been near him.

One Saturday night when I left my sanctuary at the end of my hour of watch, a distressed mother rang me up pleading with me to help her daughter. The child, Maureen, was three-and-a-half. She was suffering from a severe attack of pneumonia which was not responding to medical treatment. The doctors and the specialists who had been called in were extremely worried. The infant's temperature was dangerously high, her breathing difficult and she was tossing in pain, unable to sleep. The mother was alone with her. She was an only child and the father, a sailor, was at sea. My first impulse was to take out my old car and rush to the other side of the city where Maureen lay ill, but I was guided otherwise.

I said to the mother : " Place one hand on Maureen's brow and the other on the affected lung. Leave them there for half an hour and I will go into my sanctuary and give her Absent Healing during that time. When the half hour ends ring and tell me what has happened."

The half hour in the sanctuary seemed no more than a minute.

A further five minutes passed, the mother rang again and her words were :

" As soon as I placed my hands on Maureen's brow and lung I felt the power of God passing through me to her. Gradually her breathing became much easier and she fell asleep and is still sleeping. I think her temperature is greatly reduced. All the time I felt there was another presence in the room."

I advised the tired woman to go to bed and have a sleep and ring me again in the morning. She did this, telling me that Maureen had slept soundly all night and she thought her temperature was normal. I never heard from that mother again, but six months later I happened to pass their street and thought it would be nice to call and find out what had happened. I did not know the house number and had to search until I found it. A man came to the door and told me he now was the tenant. He did not know anything about Maureen or her mother except that now they were in Egypt with the father. It is strange, however, how things come about.

Another six months passed. I was asked to go to a house in another part of the city, far from Maureen's home, to help a young business woman, Josephine by name, who was dying of cancer. After a service the pain disappeared but I had to return every night and give a service to enable her to get natural sleep. Josephine was a wonderful Christian lady. She had been in charge of a Wolf Cub group and while lying

THE GREATEST PRIVILEGE 97

there, slowly dying, still had those little boys coming
to the house for instruction. She had many friends
who came to see her, indeed many whom she scarcely
knew visited her for she was a radiant character.
When one business lady who had never spoken to her
except by phone, heard she was dying she called, and
Josephine told her that I was giving her services. The
lady replied by telling the full story of Maureen,
whom she knew. Josephine delighted me by giving
the full details of Maureen's recovery.

When the doctors had called on the Sunday morning to see Maureen, wondering if she were still alive,
they were surprised to find her better and her temperature normal. They suspected that she had picked up
some unusual germ, so they took her to hospital for
testing purposes but soon she was back home again.

When I am asked to give Absent Healing to those
whom I cannot see I send them a healing prayer with
instructions as follows :

" Dear Friend, amongst the hundreds of letters that
have reached me appealing for the Ministry of Healing, I find your one for which I thank you sincerely.
I am most profoundly impressed by the evidence of a
deep faith in God's love and power as revealed
through Jesus Christ, a faith which has obviously
impelled the most terribly afflicted ones in the country
to appeal to me for this Divine Healing. You will
understand that it is utterly impossible for me to give
services to all who need them. I cannot, like Jesus
say, ' come unto me all ye ', I can only say come
unto me some of you but I can say to the rest of you
—go to your own ministers.

" It may comfort you, however, to know that you

may have Divine Healing for body, mind and spirit direct without any intermediary but Jesus Christ. Through Him God can mediate his healing power to you and to help you to put yourself in the way of receiving this power for yourself or dear one, I would ask you to join with me in prayer any time between eleven and twelve o'clock p.m., during which time I am in my sanctuary remembering those who need this special help.

"Do not keep yourself awake for this special purpose, however, as the healing grace can be extended to you or your dear ones while asleep. To make it easier for you to engage in this exercise of Spiritual Healing through Jesus Christ, I enclose a short prayer which you may use if necessary. Here it is :

"Father of all health and healing, a needy suppliant, I come to Thee. For all that Thou hast enabled man to do for me I offer my sincere thanks. For the knowledge, skill and tender ministries of surgeon, doctors and nurses, I praise Thee. For the measure of relief from pain and improvement in my condition I glorify Thy name. And now into Thy hands and power I commit myself for the perfecting of the good work begun. Let Thy love triumph in me and Thy power prevail in me, that Thy glory may be manifest in my healing, Thy truth in my restoration through Jesus Christ, Our Lord."

Some very wonderful results have come from this method of Absent Healing. Here is a copy of a letter from the minister of one of our Cathedral towns.

"I want to make a report regarding Miss M. A. about whom I wrote you some weeks ago. I am very happy to say she is very much better. She started to improve a month ago. Prior to that she could not go upstairs and had to be helped out of her chair. This afternoon I met her out for a short walk. She told me she had not felt so well for a whole year as she does at present.

" She is eating and has recovered her spirits. I asked her if she was still using the prayer you sent and am glad to know she repeats it every night. It is a great joy to me to be able to make this report to you with grateful thanks and heartfelt prayer for the work you are doing."

A still more strange law in connection with Absent Healing is that the patient need not know it is being given, nor need the ministering one know the name or address of either the patient or the friends who make the appeal. Here is a letter with neither address nor name in it which speaks for itself, only the date is given 1/11/53.

" Some time ago we wrote asking if you would be so good as to remember a girl, weary suffering from a severe breakdown caused by bereavement. This is just to say she has now walked out of it and is going from strength to strength. With gratitude, grateful friends."

The explanation of the above is that the Holy Spirit Who is the operative agent, knows all about such a case and where the need is real and the appeal even by anonymous friends, is sincere, He does His mighty works.

There is nothing in this to satisfy the critical medical mind that this girl's nervous breakdown was cured through prayer and my Absent Healing services. But there is enough in it to satisfy those of us who believe. Such responses happen too often to be mere coincidence.

CHAPTER 9

SURRENDERED MEN

The question arises : Who can exercise this ministry? The answer usually given is " Only those who have the gift and it is given only to certain people ". This answer is wrong. Our Lord laid down the law on the point when He said : " These signs shall follow them that believe . . . they shall lay hands on the sick and they shall recover " (Mark 16, vv. 17-18). Note the words " them that believe ". These are the limiting words. The mistake in the customary answer to the question derives from a misunderstanding of the true nature of the healing ministry.

The ministry is not the exercise of a gift we possess, but the practice of a capacity that we develop. Only the Holy Spirt can develop this capacity in any man or woman.

It is a capacity to receive and transmit the Healing Grace of God. Those who give themselves to it become receiving and transmitting instruments of the Divine Power. The conditions that further the necessary spiritual development are set out in the account already given of my own approach to the work. I must emphasise the methods of spiritual discipline.

First and supremely one must surrender to God Who by His Holy Spirit pardons, cleanses and sanctifies. Now being human and weak we cannot surrender ourselves properly; we only can offer ourselves; we must leave it to God to seize us. We must be willing to be possessed by Him and if we persist in offering ourselves He, in His own time, will take us in no doubtful fashion. He will let us know it through a baptism of the Holy Spirit.

Jesus said : " If ye then being evil know how to give good gifts unto your children, how much more shall your Heavenly Father give the Holy Spirit to them that ask Him " (Luke 11, v. 13). According to the Bible, when this happens we are sealed as God's instruments and never again can doubt.

The second essential is a regular " Hour of Watch " with Christ, during which we practise the consciousness of the Divine Presence. This spiritual discipline develops, in some measure at least, a sense of unity with God. Jesus developed this to perfection and it may be that was the essence of his divinity.

In a sense all ministers of the Gospel are surrendered men. Indeed, who is a surrendered man if it is not he who has given his whole time, strength, and potential of body, mind and soul to the work of the Kingdom of God ? I believe therefore that all ministers are close to the point of graduating for the Healing Ministry. Only one thing stands in their way, and that is a sense of their unworthiness. The Church has left them —as it is never satisfied until it has left us all—with a guilt complex. And this is wrong. It should teach us to cherish the complex of the pardoned, the redeemed, the regenerate. " All our righteousness is as filthy rags," was a strange cry on the part of Isaiah. The slightest degree of righteousness in Christians is the work of the Holy Spirit. And the Holy Spirit is not a merchant dealing in filthy rags. Besides, the Church teaches that we can claim Christ's righteousness as our own—so why hesitate ?

How many of my brother ministers have said to

me : " I do not feel in the least that I am called to the Ministry of Healing ". My answer is " it is not what you *feel* in the call of Christ that matters, but what you *hear*. And what you hear is this : ' preach the Gospel, heal the sick '."

My contention that all ministers can take up the work is verified by the history of the Glasgow Group of Ministers.

I will give here an account of the origin, activities and achievements of these dedicated men. After I had been exercising the ministry, quietly within my own congregation, for four years, I heard that a class of Divine Healing was being conducted in Community House. One of our ministers, the Reverend Fred Smith, then of Alexandria, now of Westerton, Bearsden, had organised the class. I attended, hoping to give Mr. Smith and his members the benefit of my practical experience. I found some fifteen to twenty persons, consisting chiefly of ladies of varying ages, with one or two laymen and usually three ministers. In those days I was not convinced of the wisdom of admitting women and laymen to the work and I was certain that if Mr. Smith limited himself to the field represented by the class he never would persuade ministers to take it up; so I suggested he start a class for ministers only. This he did and in a short time a group of us met in Community House every Monday for prayer, meditation, discussion and mutual encouragement and guidance, our only text book being the Bible.

At meeting after meeting I related my experiences, but when I suggested all ministers could do the work, my colleagues were doubtful, although sufficiently convinced to suggest that we hold a healing service in one of our churches and I should conduct it.

To hold a public healing service was contrary to my idea of the way the work should be done. So it was decided that to avoid undue publicity, those who had long organised prayer groups to intercede for the sick, should invite people on their prayer lists to attend for healing. But no one needing help would be excluded. Thus the service, at least, would be semi-private.

I submitted to the wisdom of the group and gave a service with results I need not relate, but my colleagues were sufficiently impressed to resolve to hold such a service once a month in our various churches in turn. These still are carried on and the patients ministered to testify to the benefits they receive.

Our first service was held in St. James's Church, Pollok, where the Rev. J. Clarence Finlayson, then was minister. After that service Clarence asked me to accompany him on visits to four of his sick members. I accepted on condition that I give each of the patients three weekly services, after which he would carry on himself. After the first round of services my friend said : " I have seen miracles this day."

When I gave a second service to one of these patients, a man suffering from a lung condition, I suddenly asked Clarence to assist by laying his hands too on the man. To my friend's surprise the patient gave the same response to his touch as to mine : thus another recruit entered the ranks. Soon the whole group was engaged in the work, true servants of Jesus Christ, transmitters of the healing power of God.

Thus my belief was strengthened that all ministers who fulfil the conditions are able to give healing services. This was further verified by four young ministers, the Rev. Griffith J. Owens of Dundyvan Parish, Coatbridge, the Rev. Thomas Lithgow, of Auchtermuchty, the Rev. James Hall of Tranent, and the Rev. Herbert K. Neil, Port of Menteith, who after attending my clinic for observation began to assist me and now can proceed with confidence on their own. Results testify to their effectiveness.

These successes raise the question whether the power to heal is part of our ordination endowment, but as we are not taught to believe in this and do not expect it, the power does not make itself manifest.

I am convinced, that in the intention of Our Lord it is so. Just as He, when in the flesh, gave His disciples power to heal all manner of sickness and all manner of disease, so to-day He would do the same through His body the Church, if the Church had the necessary faith to make it possible for Him to do so. Just as at Nazareth he did not do mighty works because of unbelief, so to-day He is restrained from this mighty work of imparting healing power to ministers at their ordination because of the unbelief of His Church.

When the group began the work and went about proclaiming the truth and reality of Baptism of the Power of the Holy Ghost, intellectual circles at Glasgow University dubbed them the "Lunatic Fringe". To-day the attitude of many of those former sceptics would be more correctly conveyed in the quotation : "They who came to scoff, remained to pray."

To show how effective the members of the Glasgow Healing Group are in extending Divine Healing to sufferers at their monthly service, I will quote from a letter, dated the 3rd of March, 1960, received from one who was marvellously helped at a group service.

" You will, I know, rejoice and give thanks with me on the wonderful healing received at the service on Monday. The acute attack of rheumatism in neck and left arm from which I suffered constant pain the past six weeks, day and night, is completely gone. The easing of the pain during the laying on of hands in addition to the great peace experienced, was sufficient proof of God's power to heal. There followed a further improvement the next day. To be able to use the arm, even a little, was a joy but more wonderful still on Wednesday I could use it normally and pain and fear were gone. I shall never cease to marvel and give thanks to all the members of the Healing Group."

In course of time and the experience it brings I should write that I have found it necessary to broaden my view that healing in the name and power of Jesus Christ should be limited to ministers. In 1952 I started an open clinic in my church prayer room in order to meet an overwhelming call for services. In those early days my wife helped me but the time came when domestic circumstances made it impossible for her to continue. Members of the group quickly came to my aid but as they were overburdened with work, I could not depend on their attendance. Then the Lord made new arrangements by sending a minister's widow to the clinic. This lady had offered herself for this work and by prayer and supplication had done much to prepare herself for it. When she consulted her own minister on the matter, he brought her to me and asked me to give her further guidance.

At the time, in my heart, I was reluctant as I was sure that none but ministers should be encouraged in this direction. But as she was the widow of the Reverend William Davidson who had been my friend, I felt I could not say no.

At first Mrs. Davidson observed the work, then she began to assist and in three months' time she was able to conduct services. Soon her work became known and to-day she answers constant appeals for help. These mean endless visits to homes to impart the blessing. This she does in addition to the working in my clinic. I am endlessly indebted to her and am glad of this opportunity to acknowledge her services.

In further proof of my contention that the limits as to those who can do this work were set by Our Lord when He said: "Them that believe", I can add that a session clerk in an East End church has undergone the same round of preparation and development and to-day is engaged in the Healing Ministry in his own congregation and district.

But, I feel I should write that, despite the selfless work of these good people, while no believing Christian, man or woman, should be debarred from undertaking the ministry, I believe that ministers should prove the most effective instruments of the Healing Power imparted by Jesus Christ. They are, after all, entirely set apart for the work of Christ's Kingdom.

Through the influence of the Glasgow Group of Healing Ministers there are many more ministers than most people are aware working quietly in the homes of their people. Many more would like to do it but lack sufficient faith in themselves as instruments in the Lord's hands.

CHAPTER 10

"ALL HIS CREATURES"

One of the most alarming features of to-day's health situation is the vast number of men and women, who suffer from nervous disorders, neuroses, phobias, etc. The first appeal such persons make is—understandably—to the medical profession. This may mean hospital treatment or resort to psychoanalysts and psychiatrists. Excellent results often are achieved and many cures are effected, but it is significant that many victims of the illnesses appeal, perforce, almost as a last resort, to the Ministry of Divine Healing. We who exercise the ministry are neither qualified psychoanalysts nor psychiatrists; but we are instruments of a Divine Agency that is all-knowing and all-powerful. Scores of such sufferers have come for the help only the Holy Spirit can impart and I cannot remember any who had the necessary faith and patience being turned away disappointed. In these cases the sufferers' patience is as essential as their faith because a long series of services usually is required. A learned professor recently said that he had never come across a single case of a person suffering from a neurosis or any similar trouble who had been helped or cured by this ministry. Obviously he had little experience of Divine Healing or knowledge of it.

Here is an excerpt from a letter sent by a doctor's wife. The lady, suffering from a neurosis, was on the point of going abroad to join her husband. She visited me twice but did not divulge that her husband was a doctor. The letter speaks for itself:

"I thought you would like to know how much better I am feeling after the two services you have given me. Since I saw you on Friday I have had no palpitation at all and have been able to sleep without pills. For over a month I took four capsules a day, but now I no longer take any and feel much stronger. Also my feeling of sickness has gone and my appetite is normal again. This is such a relief as I had been dreading the strain of these last few days before my departure. Now I feel strengthened and ready to undertake the work I must do over there. I used to be afraid to go out for fear of having attacks of nerves and hysteria, but I no longer have them. If this is not a miracle I don't know what it is. My husband is a doctor but when I tell him about this I don't think he will be sceptical. It is wonderful to think of what suffering you must ease . . ."

This case of neurosis required only two services; the malady had not been in existence long and therefore was not deep-seated. Had it been of greater duration it might have required more services. The Lord requires time to work through us on troubles of long-standing.

A case I always shall remember with happiness, because it brought relief to a whole family, was concerned with a violent neurosis. The sick man was the father of the family and I shall call him Donald. An ex-soldier, Donald had been taken by the Germans in battle and the burden of life in the prisoner-of-war camp to which he was assigned weighed heavily on his mind and spirit. He was a good man and accustomed to the ways of his own little hardworking seg-

ment of society and the long brooding in the alien
camp, away from the only way of life he knew—and
which he loved—seemed to have permanently disturbed him.

After the war he returned to his family, took up his
job again and all would have been well, but for his
state of health. He lost his appetite for food, could
not sleep, became most irritable and this nervous ir-
ritation steadily increased till he had violent outbursts
of wild temper. He had to stop working and the
enforced idleness worsened his condition. The poor
lad was living on pills. His wife too became affected
by the tension his moods created in the home. He
seemed to have no control of himself at all and eventu-
ally, in spasms of violent irrationality, would strike his
child. This was too much for the wife, who, indeed,
had been living in fear of him. One evening after
divine service she came and told me her troubles,
asking my help.

I went along to see Donald and found he had
already degenerated into a very bad *physical* state;
apart from the nervous disorder, a carbuncle had
broken out on his shoulder, and, fiercely swelling, was
causing him intense pain. We chatted awhile and
then I gave him a healing service which had instantaneous results. His interest in food quickly revived
and he sat down at the table and ate heartily of his
supper. Shortly afterwards the carbuncle burst; it was
drained; it closed and began to heal. Donald became
a new man, or rather the old happy man of his care-
free pre-soldiering days. His health restored, physically
and mentally, he went back to his job and he and his
good wife and family now are restored to the easy-
going happiness of normal family life.

Such experiences lift a man's heart.

It is more difficult to deal with psychotic cases. These cases of definite insanity assume various forms and varying degrees of intensity. They require weekly services, maybe for years. An old lady of eighty in my congregation developed a mental condition in which she suffered from delusions. One such delusion was that the Devil was going to take her minister from her and she claimed to have seen his Satanic Majesty digging a grave in the front garden in which I was to be buried alive. Accompanying such delusions was the belief that she herself was a child of the Devil and could never go to church again. She was, in fact, one of God's saints who had been a true mother in Israel, to use a Bible term. She and her family believed in the ministry of healing. It required about a dozen weekly services to cure her but she was cured, and able to go to church again and live a few more years enjoying perfect mental clarity.

Some eight years ago a friend asked me if I could do anything to help a lady who for some nineteen years had suffered from schizophrenia and for most of that time was in a mental hospital undergoing the best treatment available with little response. The approval of the hospital authorities was secured and a room was set apart where we could give the patient a private service every Thursday. Each service lasted about half an hour. The patient's mother and brother usually accompanied me. We began under difficulties due to which the first service did not take place; when we were about to start the patient took fright and bolted from the room. We let her be, leaving the task of stilling her fears to the Lord. At an appointed hour on the following Thursday we returned and found that

He had done so, preparing her in a manner known only to Himself for the service which she accepted with meek submission.

Every Thursday we went, week after week, month after month, year after year, and improvement, while very slow, was very real. At last after six years of our ministries the patient was able to leave hospital and take up a post of responsibility.

In the later years of the treatment of that lady less frequent services were required and, of course, all the time we were giving the services the hospital staff still were doing their best for her. But surely it was more than mere coincidence that improvement started with the services.

I will give one more case history in reply to statements which imply that Divine Healing is ineffective in cases of mental disorder.

Anne, the daughter of a professional gentleman, was a Mongol and a pupil at a special school for handicapped children when her father and mother brought her to my house. After the fourth service the mother told me, with hope in her eyes, that Anne's teacher had reported that the child was improving, indeed that the doctors said she had begun to develop along natural lines. The parents brought their daughter for two more services and then stopped without explanation. Later I discovered they had emigrated and apparently been too busy with the problems of their new life to find time to explain why they stopped bringing Anne to me.

But the story does not end there. Three years later I was invited by a Glasgow councillor, a member of the Committee on Special Schools, to accompany him to a picnic given by the City Corporation to the pupils of these schools. Every year during the first week of June, some twenty buses take hundreds of handicapped little souls to Balloch Park on the banks of Loch Lomond and they are given a glorious day of entertainment. Every day during the week these busloads go to the park (which is one of Glasgow's smoke-free lungs) until every handicapped child has been given a fresh air outing by the beautiful loch. The presence of these afflicted children with their teachers working themselves to exhaustion in their determination to give their pathetic little pupils at least one day of happiness in the year, adds to the beauty of the scene a radiance which nature herself cannot impart.

I walked round the park, visiting each school-party and was struck with special interest when I came to a group of Mongols. Halting there I chatted to the headmistress who had been in charge of the school for many years. I asked if in her experience any Mongol child had ever become normal. " In all my experience," she replied, " I have only had one child who became normal. Her name was Anne and it was the most marvellous thing I have ever seen. No other child in my long experience has so recovered."

She did not give me the second name of that child, neither did I tell her that I knew it but I told God I was grateful.

I have no doubt that some of the things I have written in previous chapters have shocked many whose faith does not go the length of this ministry. I pray that these next few lines especially do not shock them further : to me these experiences add depth to the work of the Healing Ministry.

When I started the work I received a letter from a critic who said he did not believe in the ministry because it did not apply to animals. At the time I had neither the knowledge nor experience to reply. Now I can and my answer is, yes it does apply to animals. In September, 1955, a Glasgow minister asked if I would try to help his son, a lad of ten, who was suffering from catarrh in the head. The trouble was spoiling the boy's powers of concentration and hindering his progress at school. I agreed to see him and went to his father's manse every Sunday night after my day's ordinary work was completed.

On Christmas Day, when I made my visit I found that the minister himself was ill and his wife took me to his room. At the foot of his bed I noticed, partly under the quilt, his son's pet dog, an animal about half the size of a collie. The poor creature, I was told, was suffering from distemper and it seemed nearly dead. It was unable to stand, could scarcely lift its head, was suffering intense pain all over its body and if touched it snapped and snarled. As the lady of the manse and I stood looking at it she said to me:

" Mr. Peddie, John told me to ask if you'd give Ollie a service of Divine Healing as he is sure that Jesus would heal him just as well as He had healed himself."

The little boy's faith shamed me. I had never thought of such a thing but I could not refuse. God was going to enlarge my knowledge and experience of the ministry through the boy and his dying dog. But I did not know how to go about the task. I could not pick up a Bible and say: " Little dog hear the Word of God "; neither could I ask the creature to join me in prayer. But I simply had to give Ollie a service so, as usual, I surrendered myself to the Divine Power and prayed in silence, stretching out to put my hands on his head. Apprehensively, I felt he might snap but he lay still, I stroked his head and he neither snapped nor snarled. I stroked his spine, still no objections. I stroked his four legs, and he fell asleep.

After I gave the minister a service, then John a service, it was nearly midnight and we had a cup of tea. We had just finished when Ollie came crawling from under the quilt on to the edge of the bed. His mistress, fearing he might fall and hurt himself, lifted and carried him to her kitchen and laid him on the floor. In the most lively way he began to prance about and finally came bouncing upstairs, back into the bedroom, jumping and licking our hands.

A few days later the lady took him to her veterinary surgeon who when she saw him exclaimed in surprise : " But this is miraculous. This is a miracle."

I have had other experiences of the kind. For example, about a year ago I went to a suburb of Glasgow to minister to a lady. She and her husband have a dog, Taffy, of which they are fond and he of them. He is a pedigree Golden Labrador and this particular night was lying on the floor unable to get on to his feet. They asked me if I could help him and I reassured them. It was their pet's hind legs, they said, that were affected and, as a consequence, he could not stand. In silent prayer I laid my hands on his haunches and thighs, ending by stroking them gently and, in a few minutes he was on his feet, and able to take a walk with his master.

Here is a case that happened in my own home where not so long ago a canine-feline duel, so to speak, compelled me to undertake a similar service. We have a large black dog, Lindy, a cross between a Labrador and a collie. She is young and full of life, and we also have a black cat, a sharp-tempered creature, that can make a dog run. His name is Sooty. One day Sooty was asleep on Lindy's chair. Naturally the dog did not approve and foolishly jumped up to dislodge him. Out slashed Sooty's claws and tore right across Lindy's eye. It became opaque and our poor pet obviously was blind in that eye. A doctor pronounced it permanently useless, but that night I gave Lindy a service, keeping my hand about an inch away from the eye lest I hurt it. For another two nights I repeated this service and on the fourth day to the surprise of the household (who did not know I had given her services), her eye was perfectly restored and without a mark of any kind.

God loves His whole creation and what He does for men He does for all His creatures, making His Healing Grace available to all. Surely we may expect as much from a God Who, according to Jesus, marks the sparrow's fall.

CHAPTER II

THE LAWS OF HEALING

The inquiring and perhaps sceptical reader will ask about failures?

What, they may say, of those who get no benefit and are left to suffer in discomfort, pain and mental agony till the end?

The answer is that in this ministry there are no complete failures. Everyone who is sincere in his seeking and is prepared patiently to wait upon God, receives a blessing mental and spiritual, if not physical, to an exceptional degree and doctors admit this is so. It is seldom that pain does not yield and when it does not, something within the power of the surgeon or doctor or hospital staff is required, as I have stated. There are cases, of course, where the sufferer has "fallen in love" with his trouble and for various reasons does not wish relief. A person like this continues to ask for services because he receives comfort from the Holy Spirit, but still he clings to his afflictions —real or imaginary. We never turn away such persons but gladly minister to them in the hope and belief that the Power we serve one day will remove the mental obstacles which stand in the way of complete recovery.

Another aspect of apparent failure arises because so relatively few are doing the work. Constant appeals come to us, some so pathetic we find it impossible to refuse. An appeal may mean travelling considerable distances and the trouble may be of a type that requires a long series of services, and in certain circumstances this may be impossible. A consequence of this may be that the patient will feel we have failed him. But when all ministers take up the work, as some day they must, this charge of failure will be untenable. It will be a great day when the Church's spiritual life becomes so intense, and its faith so firm and deep that every minister who does not take up the work will be obsessed with a sense of failure in face of his Master's commission : " Preach the Gospel; heal the sick." It will be a still greater day when the capacity to exercise the ministry will be a compulsory qualification for admission to our holy calling.

We pray for the time when theological colleges will have chairs of Divine Healing. The occupant of that chair, instead of sharpening the intellects of students by hammering into them the theories and ideas of, say, Karl Heim, Rudolf Bultmann, Karl Barth, Sören Kierkegaard, Martin Heidegger, Oscar Cullmann, Karl Jaspers, Paul Tillich and all the rest of that galaxy of intellectual stars, familiarity with whose works may prove a mark of culture and theological erudition, will impart the Secret of the Kingdom of God which Jesus entrusted to His disciples. That secret throws wide the " everlasting doors " of the personality for the entrance of that Holy Spirit and His power which Jesus promised.

I suggest, in other words, that while the attainment of the highest possible ethical and intellectual standards must not be neglected, the development of the spiritual faculties latent in every person, should be man's paramount aim in life. When that happens there will be fewer charges of neglect or failure brought against the clergy.

As I look back across the years I have been engaged

in healing work, I recall only one occasion on which I could pronounce my effort a complete failure. It was indeed, more than a failure, for it has left something in my soul that keeps repeating in an accusing tone: "You could have done better."

It was midnight, just when my Hour of Watch had ended that a father whose heart was breaking, telephoned and asked if I would come to his house to help his daughter who was ill of a heart attack. I went, he met me at his front door and his first words told me he did not know whether the girl's illness was terminal; but it appeared to be. I was shown to the sick room where the mother was waiting, an expression of agony on her face. Curled in bed, her head under the blankets, was their child, a charming young lady of about twenty. She herself was interested in every good work among the young and ready to spend her time and strength in their service. As I gazed at her I felt absolutely helpless and if my faith did not fail me, my courage did.

To move her and lay one hand on her head and the other on her heart, which I ought to have done might, I feared, be dangerous.

I know now that it would not. In this work God never will allow anything to hurt His servant. But at that time I lacked experience. So I merely laid my hands on the bed-covering and prayed.

I know now that I should have gone about the Father's business in a more businesslike manner and while I cannot say that if I had done so the girl would have recovered, I am sure I would have helped her more. The Divine Power did not fail on that occasion. I failed. So whispers the accusing voice within.

I am aware that the Power that operates in the

Ministry provides a most interesting subject for study and investigation. I would welcome sincere students.

The first and last word, I know, regarding Divine Healing rests of course with our Lord. We read that when He still was in the flesh He gave His disciples power to heal all manner of sickness and all manner of disease and was able to impart the necessary power directly to them. In a final interview with His friends before His ascension, He said: " Ye shall receive power, after that the Holy Ghost is come upon you, and ye shall be witnesses unto me." These words imply that the power is to be imparted through the Holy Spirit, but quite clearly is not to be identified with that spirit. It is a different entity. This is further confirmed by Peter, when in a sermon (recorded in Acts, 10) he said: " God anointed Jesus of Nazareth with the Holy Ghost and with Power." There is definitely a differentiation there between the Holy Ghost and the Power.

What is this power? In Hebrews 6, it is referred to in the plural—the powers of the world to come. Here too, there is association with the Holy Spirit. The author is speaking of those who were partakers of the Holy Ghost and as a result have tasted the powers of the world to come. This Jesus named as the Kingdom of Heaven. It is a mistake to interpret that phrase as meaning an ideal state of society that shall one day be established upon the earth. If that ever happens it will not be the Kingdom of Heaven but the effect of the influence of the powers of that kingdom. We recall Christ's words to Pilate: " My kingdom is not of this world."

Now it is with the powers of the kingdom that we are dealing in this Healing Ministry. To adopt more modern terms we may call that kingdom the Spiritual Universe. It is just as real to those who inhabit it as this material universe is to us. Indeed, I would go so far as to say that those inhabitants of earth who under the power of the Holy Spirit develop their spiritual faculties, can at times perceive its reality. As Paul says: "These things are spiritually discerned." In my opinion this was what Jesus was referring to when He said to His disciples: "It is given unto you to know the mysteries of the Kingdom of Heaven." And again: "Many prophets and righteous men have desired to see those things which ye see and have not seen them."

I am confident that Jesus spent much time in training the disciples to develop their latent spiritual faculties against the task that lay ahead. I know that it is possible to interpret these sayings of Our Lord at the ethical and material level, but it gives His message a richer significance when we interpret them at the spiritual level.

The Kingdom of Heaven has as great a variety of Divine Energy as this material universe has, and these forms of divine power have all been made available by the Creator to meet the needs of the children of men. They are mediated through Jesus Christ and the Holy Spirit has a part to play.

What part the Holy Spirit plays is difficult, I know very well, to visualise, but, to resort to material terms to express spiritual truths, just as Jesus used the terms bread and water for the same purpose, one might imagine the personality of Jesus acting as a sort of resistance to adapt the volume of Divine Grace to the need and receptive powers of the patient. At any rate, it is a fact that during a service with the laying on of hands, the volume of power is modified in various ways, gradually increasing in strength and when enough has been ministered gradually decreasing until it is completely withdrawn. This is the time when the hand should be lifted and placed on another part if necessary. Then if needed the power will return. The person ministering is always conscious of the power passing through him (provided he has developed sufficient spiritual sensitivity) and the patient is aware of its presence from the strange heat or coldness that develops. The heat that results at the affected part is sometimes so intense that the patient remarks : "Oh, it's simply burning." The sense of coldness often impels the remark : " Oh, it's simply freezing." But neither the heat nor the coldness, no matter how intense, produces discomfort or pain, indeed on the contrary, there always is a feeling of being comforted and soothed.

The power operates according to definite laws. After all it is God not chaos from which it emanates. Gradually we are discovering its laws.

The first law that became evident was that where nothing is required, nothing is given.

Some people ask for a service out of sheer curiosity. For example, a spiritualist came to me one day pretending to be ill. " There's nothing in it. I could do that myself," she remarked at the close of the service. I have even been tested by two ministers who came with the same motive. They got their deserts. " God is not mocked."

A second law is that when the power expresses itself in coldness, it is nerve treatment that is being given. There is something wrong in the nervous system when this happens; and we can locate the centre of the trouble from the intensity of the power over the part affected. If it is a disorder that affects the whole nervous system, then the chilling is felt throughout the whole frame. But if it be a particular nerve or nerve centre only that is out of order, the power manifests itself more intensely, or it may be only, at the point where the disorder lies.

This law also holds with each of the many forms of manifestations which the power may assume. The sense of heat and coldness have already been noted. But there may be strange vibrations, or a feeling of having electric needles inserted or as if some mysterious fingers were manipulating or measuring the internal organs or organ. It is all very mysterious and it is very real.

May it not be that we are becoming, under God, involved in some of the mysteries of the Kingdom of Heaven about which Jesus spoke to His disciples?

However that may be, the same law operates with all aspects of this divine power. According to the intensity with which the power expresses itself one can locate the real centre of the trouble. This, I must write, *does not mean that we are able to diagnose as a doctor can*. We only can point to the *locus mali*. But in our work we have, at least, one advantage over the radiologist. We cannot apply too much power and harm the patient. The Mind that knows and the Hand that controls withdraws the power when enough has been applied.

Another law I have discovered is that among the variety of Divine Powers we deal with, there is one form that does not register in the conscious mind. I learned this from a patient who was a victim of angina of effort.

With his doctor's permission this man came to me for services and with the benefit derived from them, plus his doctor's treatment, he experienced definite improvement. During a service he told me he always was conscious of a sense of heat or coldness with almost regular alternation—one service characterised by heat the next by coldness. But occasionally, he said, he was conscious of neither, only a sense of soothing. The strange thing was, he received or seemed to receive as much benefit on the latter occasions as on the former. This seems to suggest that there is a powerful type of healing emanation that does not register in the mind of the patient. This may perhaps be due to the fact that it is of too high or too low a frequency. It also may explain why there is a considerable number of people who, although they are exceptional, feel only a sense of soothing, but get as much benefit as the others.

I have ministered to several scientists and from what they experienced under such services, they all agree that the operative principle in the ministry is the radiation principle; that by surrender to the Divine Power for cleansing and sanctification we become receiving and transmitting instruments of a healing "ray". From the strange sense of activity that goes on in the frontal lobes of my brain during a service, a sense of activity that is most intense about the middle of the forehead, I would even say that some of my brain cells act as receiving and transmitting valves for the divine " rays " of healing love and grace. The learned may say that in so thinking and speaking I am reducing what is purely spiritual to the level of the material. Quite the opposite; I am raising the material to the level of the spiritual. In the last analysis this material creation of God is fundamentally spiritual.

We now approach the conclusion of the whole matter. It is this. This ministry of Divine Healing really is a science conceived and made possible by the only comprehensive and unerring scientist in existence —the Divine Creator. By His foresight and planning and creative power He made wireless, television and all the other thrilling aspects of modern civilisation possible. But He also devised, planned and created an instrument, the human personality, capable of " tuning in " for personal benefit, to the rays of His redeeming love. Thus it is able to pick up the healing rays that radiate from His throne and transmit them to all in need.

APPENDIX

THE GLASGOW GROUP

I should like to acknowledge here the inspiration and generous help and encouragement given me by the following Ministers, my friends and colleagues of the Glasgow Group, who are now carrying out and, under God, perpetuating the work of Divine Healing throughout Scotland.

Rev. Frederick A. Smith, M.A., B.A., Westerton Parish, Bearsden, the Leader of the Group; Rev. J. Clarence Finlayson, M.A., Minister of Grange Parish, Edinburgh, and Leader of The Christian Fellowship of Healing (Scotland), 24 Ainsley Place, Edinburgh; Rev. A. J. O. Gordon, M.A., Toryglen Parish, who also conducts by correspondence a Healing Ministry entitled " The Kingdom Way "; Rev. John R. Ramsay, B.D., Mount Florida Parish (deceased); Rev. Paul B. Hilton, Kerse Parish, Grangemouth; Rev. Nigel A. M. MacKenzie, St. Mary's Parish, Aberdeen; Rev. Alexander Y. Struthers, M.A., Drumblade Parish, Huntly, Aberdeenshire; Rev. Edwin Lowe, B.D., North Parish, Saltcoats; Rev. Robert B. McVicar, M.A., Davidson's Mains, Edinburgh; Rev. A. Scott Donaldson, Trinity Parish, Campsie, Glasgow; Rev. Alan Boyd Robson, M.A., Kelvinside Botanic Gardens Parish, who conducts a public service for Divine Healing every Wednesday evening; Rev. W. H. Rogan, M.A., B.D., Paisley Abbey, who conducts a Divine Healing Clinic in the Abbey every Saturday evening; Rev. John B. Skelly, Renfrew Old Parish; Rev.

George K. M. Mortimer, Houston and Killellan Parish; Rev. John H. Hamilton, Yoker Old Parish; Rev. John W. Blair, Glencairn Parish, Dumfries; Rev. Frank W. Rae, B.D., Cardonald Parish, Glasgow; Rev. Alexander M. Duff, St. Andrew Parish, Penilee; Rev. Charles W. Miller, M.A., Munro Parish, Rutherglen.

THE PLAIN MAN LOOKS AT THE LORD'S PRAYER
WILLIAM BARCLAY
The historical background to and the precise meaning of the
Lord's Prayer.

THE PLAIN MAN'S BOOK OF PRAYERS
WILLIAM BARCLAY
Written specially for Fontana by a distinguished scholar and
gifted preacher to help those who wish to pray.

MORE PRAYERS FOR THE PLAIN MAN
WILLIAM BARCLAY
An essential companion to *The Plain Man's Book of Prayers*,
containing slightly longer daily prayers and Bible readings.

THE PLAIN MAN LOOKS AT THE BEATITUDES
WILLIAM BARCLAY
In working out the implications of the startling paradoxes of
the Beatitudes, the author helps to discover the technique of
being a Christian.

LETTERS AND PAPERS FROM PRISON
DIETRICH BONHOEFFER
These documents, smuggled out of prison under the nose of the
Gestapo, have a clear and shining unity.

GOD'S FROZEN PEOPLE
MARK GIBBS AND T. RALPH MORTON
'A most important and stimulating book . . . clear and revolu-
tionary thinking about the role of the laity.'
                                    ARCHDEACON OF LONDON

THE MAN NEXT TO ME
ANTHONY BARKER
'An altogether exceptional exposition of modern missionary
endeavour.'   TREVOR HUDDLESTON